SAMS
Teach Yourself

Exchange
Server 2003

in 10 Minutes

James V. Walker

SAMS *800 East 96th Street, Indianapolis, Indiana, 46240 USA*

Sams Teach Yourself Exchange Server 2003 in 10 Minutes

Copyright © 2006 by Sams Publishing

International Standard Book Number: 0-672-32724-4

Library of Congress Catalog Card Number: 2004096711

Printed in the United States of America

First Printing: November 2005

08   07   06   05   4   3   2   1

Trademarks

Warning and Disclaimer

Bulk Sales

Sams Publishing offers excellent discounts on this book when ordered in quantity for bulk purchases or special sales. For more information, please contact

> **U.S. Corporate and Government Sales**
> **1-800-382-3419**
> corpsales@pearsontechgroup.com

For sales outside of the U.S., please contact

> **International Sales**
> international@pearsoned.com

PUBLISHER
Paul Boger

ACQUISITIONS EDITOR
Neil Rowe

DEVELOPMENT EDITOR
Songlin Qiu

MANAGING EDITOR
Charlotte Clapp

SENIOR PROJECT EDITOR
Matthew Purcell

COPY EDITOR
Barbara Hacha

INDEXER
Aaron Black

PROOFREADER
Leslie Joseph

TECHNICAL EDITOR
Paul Clement

PUBLISHING COORDINATOR
Cindy Teeters

DESIGNER
Gary Adair

PAGE LAYOUT
Nonie Ratcliff

Table of Contents

Part I Exchange Server 2003 Overview

1 Introducing Exchange Server 2003   5

PART IV   Performance, Optimization, and Disaster Recovery Techniques

12   Performance Monitoring, Optimizing, and Troubleshooting   162

13   Backing Up Data Stores with the Windows Server 2003 Backup Utility   175

About the Author

James V. Walker, MCSE, CPM, BSME—James Walker has been in the information technology industry for more than 20 years and has been a contributing author, technical editor, and technical reviewer for a number of books involving security, electronic messaging, network operating systems, and data communications. As director of engineering for Pandora Networks (an XoIP On Demand Communications company), James is involved in the technology selection, design, planning, implementation, and troubleshooting of collaboration and presence IT projects for Fortune 500 companies. After years of supporting Microsoft-based technologies, James used his experience as primary technical editor and contributing author for a number of Sams Publishing technology books, including *Microsoft Windows Server 2003 Unleashed*, *Microsoft Exchange Server 2003 Unleashed*, *Microsoft Windows Server 2003 Insider Solutions*, and *Microsoft Exchange Server 2003 Delta Guide*.

Dedication

I would like to dedicate this book to Anne, my wife, and to Malcolm and Nellie, my parents. Thank you for your loving support and guidance throughout this project.

Acknowledgments

Although my name is highlighted on the front of the book, many people worked very hard in getting this book published. Without the monumental efforts of the entire editorial and production team at SAMS, this book would not have come together as nicely as it has.

A special thanks to Neil Rowe (Acquisitions Editor) for providing me the opportunity to write this book!

I would like to thank Songlin Qiu (Development Editor), Paul Clement (Tech Editor extraordinaire), Barbara Hacha (Copy Editor), Matt Purcell (Project Editor), and everyone else who contributed behind the scenes to make my book a huge success: THANK YOU for your hard work and support to get this book finished. All book projects should run this smoothly. It was truly a pleasure working with you.

Thanks again to Anne, my wife, for gently pushing me when I didn't feel like writing. Without her support, I would still be writing!

Finally, thanks to my extended network of family, friends, and peers. Your enthusiasm and encouragement was astounding and provided energy to keep me plugging away. A special thanks to Joe Piette, MCSE and certified Microsoft instructor, for reviewing technical topics and asking key questions regarding the book content.

We Want to Hear from You!

As the reader of this book, *you* are our most important critic and commentator. We value your opinion and want to know what we're doing right, what we could do better, what areas you'd like to see us publish in, and any other words of wisdom you're willing to pass our way.

As an associate publisher for Sams Publishing, I welcome your comments. You can email or write me directly to let me know what you did or didn't like about this book—as well as what we can do to make our books better.

Please note that I cannot help you with technical problems related to the topic of this book. We do have a User Services group, however, where I will forward specific technical questions related to the book.

When you write, please be sure to include this book's title and author as well as your name, email address, and phone number. I will carefully review your comments and share them with the author and editors who worked on the book.

Email: feedback@samspublishing.com

Mail: Paul Boger
         Publisher
         Sams Publishing
         800 East 96th Street
         Indianapolis, IN 46240 USA

For more information about this book or another Sams Publishing title, visit our website at www.samspublishing.com. Type the ISBN (excluding hyphens) or the title of a book in the Search field to find the page you're looking for.

Introduction

The primary goal of this book is to provide Exchange 2003 users with a series of lessons that provide information and examples of the procedures that are most important to Exchange administrators and power users. Each lesson is designed to take about 10 minutes to read. The lessons are based on my experiences, in house and out in the field, supporting Exchange organizations of all sizes. Those experiences helped me determine what features and topics would be most useful to a broad audience. I also used feedback from end-user training participants and instructors of administrator training classes to further fine-tune the lessons.

Who Is This Book For?

This book targets three specific audiences:

- End users—Entry-level individuals who have had limited or no exposure to Exchange 2003.

- Power users—Users who have intermediate- to advanced-level knowledge of Exchange 2003.

- Exchange administrators—Individuals who are tasked with daily administration and support of Exchange 2003.

In my experience, I have found that many individuals tasked to be Exchange Administrators lack significant technical expertise and training. The early lessons in the book will be helpful in getting them "up to speed." As readers become more familiar with Exchange 2003 features and functionality, the later lessons will help them in using more advanced features.

How Is This Book Organized?

The information and examples provided in this book apply to Microsoft Exchange Server 2003 with SP1. Prior versions of Exchange—Exchange

2000 and Exchange 5.x—are not covered in this book. Administrative procedures that require a workstation were performed with Windows XP SP1+ with Internet Explorer 6.0 and all available service packs. Although other operating systems and Internet browsers can be used for administration in some cases, they may provide results and functionality different from those explained in the pages of this book.

Goals for Part I

Part I of this book is written for users who are new to Exchange or need to refresh their knowledge of Exchange 2003 Server. The part introduces the reader to Exchange 2003 by providing information on new features, removed features, installation requirements, Active Directory, and more. Ideally, these lessons will be read in order by those new to Exchange, because the information builds on itself. More experienced users will be able to browse the information for specific topics of interest.

Goals for Part II–IV

Parts II–IV of this book are geared toward individuals who have been assigned the task of administering an Exchange 2003 Server. The most common administrative tasks are detailed in the lessons in these sections.

These sections apply to individuals who are given full Exchange administrative rights, because most of the procedures described require those rights. The procedures are meant to be a guide through configuration and administrative tasks and other performance, optimization, and disaster-recovery techniques.

Although meant to be read sequentially, the lessons can be referenced individually because most of the lessons are independent of others and require minimal prerequisite steps from earlier lessons. Because of this, the lessons in this portion of the book can be used as a quick reference guide by administrators looking to perform a specific task.

Conventions Used in This Book

This book uses different typefaces to differentiate between code and regular English, and also to help you identify important concepts.

Text that you type and text that should appear on your screen is presented in monospace type.

```
It will look like this to mimic the way text looks on your
screen.
```

Placeholders for variables and expressions appear in *monospace italic* font. You should replace the placeholder with the specific value it represents.

This arrow (➡) at the beginning of a line of code means that a single line of code is too long to fit on the printed page. Continue typing all the characters after the ➡ as though they were part of the preceding line.

Note   A note represents interesting pieces of information relevant to the surrounding discussion.

Tip   A tip offers advice or teaches you an easier way to do a task or procedure.

Caution   A caution advises you about potential issues to avoid or take into account.

Headlined sidebars provide additional information and examples in more detail.

LESSON 1

Introducing Exchange Server 2003

This lesson covers new, improved, and removed features in Exchange Server 2003.

New Features

With the release of Exchange Server 2003, Microsoft has created a robust email server platform that includes many new and improved features. The improvements and enhancements are most noticeable in the areas of administration, email access, security, and reliability. Although both versions of Exchange Server 2003, Standard and Enterprise, include the improved and enhanced features, there are features specific only to Exchange Server 2003 Enterprise. Let's take a look at some of these features.

Improved Administration, Deployment, and Management Tools

Microsoft made a concerted effort to improve and enhance the administration, deployment, and migration tools in this release of Exchange. The new tools include updated wizards and user interfaces that make installing, configuring, and maintaining Exchange easier. Exchange System Manager, ExDeploy, Internet Mail Wizard, and the Active Directory Account Cleanup Wizard are a few examples of the improved tools included in Exchange 2003.

Updated Outlook Web Access

Exchange 2003 includes an updated version of Outlook Web Access (OWA) that evens the messaging playing field with the full Outlook 2003 client in terms of the look, feel, and usability of the web interface. OWA, developed in conjunction with Exchange 2003, has features that complement Exchange and allow users to access their mailboxes and public folders via their web browser. Because the interfaces are almost identical, end users will immediately be comfortable when using Outlook Web Access or Outlook 2003.

Updated VSAPI

Microsoft has included an updated version of the virus scanning application programming interface (VSAPI). Introduced in Exchange 5.5 SP3 (version 1.0) and updated in Exchange 2000 SP1 (version 2.0), VSAPI was updated to version 2.5 in Exchange 2003. VSAPI provides proactive on-demand and background monitoring of incoming email messages and their attachments for viruses, worms, Trojans, and the like. Unlike previous versions, the updated virus-scanning API (VSAPI 2.5) now includes new features that enable Exchange-aware antivirus software to run on servers that do not host mailboxes such as front-end or bridgehead servers. VSAPI also includes the capability to delete infected messages and notify senders of infected messages. These features help IT departments maintain a healthy network and allow administrators to focus on keeping users productive.

Enhanced Reliability, Backup, and Recovery via Volume Shadow Copy Service and Mailbox Recovery Center

As the code name for Exchange 2003, Titanium, suggests, Microsoft had reliability and availability in its sights when it developed its latest version of Exchange. In conjunction with its Trustworthy Computing Initiative, Exchange leverages the Windows 2003 server Volume Shadow Copy Service (VSS), which makes point-in-time snapshots of data for easier backup-and-restore functionality. The snapshots or shadow copy backups are exact copies of files or volumes at a specific point in time. After the snapshot is completed, it is backed up via a backup application. Microsoft also provides a new feature, the Mailbox Recovery Center (MRC), which makes recovering multiple deleted mailboxes easier than ever. Instead of connecting to mailboxes individually, as required in the Exchange 2000 System Manager, the MRC in Exchange 2003 allows you to connect to and recover multiple mailboxes simultaneously on one server, even if the mailboxes are located on different servers.

Exchange Server 2003 Enterprise Specific Features

In addition to the features previously covered, the Enterprise Edition of Exchange Server 2003 includes support for the following:

- Eight-node Clustering using the Windows Clustering service in Windows Server 2003 Enterprise Edition or Windows Server 2003 Datacenter Edition—Cluster support is expanded from two- and four-node support in Exchange 2000 to eight nodes in Exchange 2003. Improvements in setup and security as well as support for volume mount points are also included in Exchange 2003.

- Multiple storage groups, multiple databases, and virtually unlimited database size—Exchange 2003 Standard Edition supports a single storage group (think of a group as a container) with two databases (one mailbox store and one public folder store), and Exchange 2003 Enterprise Edition supports up to four storage groups, with each storage group containing up to five databases. This allows up to 20 individual information stores on a single Exchange 2003 Server. In addition, whereas the Exchange Server 2003 Standard Edition information stores have a maximum of 16GB, the information stores in Enterprise Edition are limited only by the hardware being used, with a theoretical limit of 16TB (terabytes) of storage. Wow! I challenge someone to top that!

- X.400 connectors—The Enterprise Edition includes an X.400 connector that can be configured to handle email in and out of an organization and supports both TCP/IP and X.25. The X.400 connector is also very useful for integrating an Exchange Server into a third-party messaging platform for coexistence between an Exchange routing group and an X.400 system or during a server migration between two Exchange routing groups.

Messaging, Collaboration, and Presence in the Enterprise

Exchange Server 2003 is the latest version of Microsoft's collaboration, presence, and messaging product. Enhancing features found in Exchange 2000, Exchange 2003 extends the messaging platform with new features and leverages the stability, reliability, and functionality of the underlying Windows Server 2003 technology. Microsoft also understands that real-time enterprise is here, and it's here to stay. Microsoft embraces today's business goals: help people work together in today's workplace, quickly and easily, whenever and wherever they need to; ensuring employees can communicate and collaborate with their peers and/or experts successfully; and cutting costs while boosting productivity. Using the new features in Outlook Web Access, Outlook Mobile Access, or Outlook 2003 and Exchange Server 2003 in conjunction with Microsoft Live Communications Server 2005 provides a complete solution for real-time, converged applications with a familiar user interface. See Part III "Exchange Server Email Clients: OWA, OMA, and Outlook 2003" in this book for information on the messaging, collaboration, and presence features of Exchange Server 2003.

Choosing an Edition

Whether you choose the Standard Edition or the Enterprise Edition of Exchange Server 2003 depends on your organization's size and the Exchange features you require. Typically, the number of users supported becomes the key reason for selecting one edition over the other; both editions have the same components, the same administration and management tools, and the same servers. Let's take a look at each of the editions.

Exchange Server 2003 Standard

Exchange Server 2003 Standard Edition incorporates the same server functionality as the Enterprise Edition: web access, mobile access, reliability, and security. The Standard Edition is primarily targeted for small- to medium-sized organizations that do not require the feature-rich enterprise-level messaging functionality required in larger organizations. For example, the server may be used as an email server for a small organization, a front-end server in a larger organization, or a bridgehead server for an Exchange organization.

As previously mentioned, Exchange 2003 Standard Edition supports a single storage group with two databases (one mailbox store and one public folder store) with an individual database size of 16GB. The database size is a limiting factor in the number of users that can be supported. Clustering support and X.400 support are also missing from this edition. Be sure to analyze your particular environment before choosing the Standard Edition for your organization.

Exchange Server 2003 Enterprise

The Enterprise Edition of Exchange Server 2003 is targeted at large and worldwide organizations that need more than a 16GB messaging database. With support for up to four storage groups, with each storage group containing up to five databases, a single Exchange 2003 Server can support up to 20 individual information stores. Unlike the Exchange Server 2003 Standard Edition, the information stores in Enterprise Edition are limited only by an organization's hardware budget and the hardware being used, with a theoretical limit of 16TB (terabytes) of storage.

Enterprise Edition also supports clustering capabilities, which allow for maximum system availability and fault tolerance—usually a top priority for large organizations with a large number of mailboxes and mail storage.

In addition, the Enterprise Edition includes an X.400 connector, which is not supported in the Standard Edition of Exchange.

Note   Although the Enterprise Edition of Exchange 2003 can work with any version of Windows 2003 or Windows 2000, clustering is available only if the Enterprise version or Datacenter Version of Windows 2000/2003 is used for the server platform. The Standard Edition does not support clustering.

Table 1.1 compares the Standard and Enterprise Editions of Exchange Server 2003.

TABLE 1.1   Exchange 2003 Standard Versus Enterprise Editions

Exchange 2003 Feature	Standard Edition	Enterprise Edition
Number of storage groups supported	1	4
Number of databases per storage group supported	2 (1 private, 1 public)	5
Maximum database size	16GB	Unlimited (16TB maximum)
Clustering support	None	Up to 8 nodes
X.400 connector support	None	Included
OS support	Windows 2000 SP3 or later or Windows Server 2003 Standard or Enterprise or Datacenter	Windows 2003 Enterprise or Datacenter

Installation Prerequisites

Although I won't be covering the installation process in detail here, several prerequisites must be performed before the installation and configuration of Exchange 2003 in an organization is initiated. Completing a preinstallation checklist will help ensure a smooth, efficient, and successful installation of Exchange Server 2003 in your organization. Let's take a look at some of the items you should review before beginning an Exchange installation.

Network Requirements

Before you start your Exchange installation, be sure that your network has a general good bill of health with a working DNS and WINS installed and configured in your domain. Double-check that your servers (domain controllers, global catalog servers in the AD topology and the domain) are running Windows 2000 SP3 or later or Windows Server 2003 and that Active Directory is healthy and is being replicated throughout your network environment without any errors. Use ExDeploy to easily verify your server health against a checklist using tools and utilities to confirm that your server and organization are ready for the Exchange 2003 installation. The Exchange Server Deployment tools and documentation are complete and easy to use and will lead you through an entire Exchange Server 2003 installation or upgrade.

 Note   The latest version of ExDeploy can be located by searching the Microsoft Download Center at http://www.microsoft.com/downloads.

Hardware

Determining the proper hardware required for your Exchange 2003 server can be tricky. You must take into consideration the organization's size and number of users, bandwidth usage, daily patterns of email usage, and the organization's requirements for messaging system availability and reliability. At a minimum, select a computer with the following components:

- Intel Pentium or compatible 133MHz or faster processor.

- 256MB RAM.

- 500MB free drive space on the disk containing Exchange 2003 (200MB system drive).

- VGA or higher resolution.

- Keyboard, mouse, or other compatible input device.

- Disk partitions must be formatted for the NTFS file system, not the FAT file system.

- CD drive.

For a single server setup or prototype/lab situation, these minimums might be fine; for large organizations they will be not be sufficient. To better gauge an organization's hardware needs, check out some of the hardware-sizing tools available for Exchange Server 2003. Unfortunately, Microsoft's Exchange Capacity Planning and Topology Calculator is no longer available, so I recommend that you use the following supported tools for help with correctly sizing your Exchange Server installation:

- The Exchange Server Load Simulator 2003 (LoadSim) tool—This tool simulates the performance load of MAPI clients and tests how a server running Microsoft Exchange Server 2003 responds to email loads.

- The Exchange Server 2003 Jetstress Tool—Useful for both Exchange Server 2003 and Microsoft Exchange 2000 Server, this tool simulates disk I/O load on a test server running Exchange Server and verifies the performance and the stability of your disk subsystem.

- Exchange Server Stress and Performance (ESP) 2003—Using this tool, administrators can simulate large numbers of client sessions by concurrently accessing one or more protocol servers; included modules simulate a variety of protocols and the loads incurred by multiple client machines.

Note In addition, because most hardware vendors work closely with Microsoft Hardware Quality Labs to endure maximum compatibility, reliability, and performance, hardware vendors such as Hewlett-Packard and Dell are able to develop their own tools that assist customers in sizing the minimum requirements for their Exchange 2003 servers. Hewlett-Packard has a seven-step web-based tool called HP Proliant Sizer for Microsoft Exchange Server 2003 (registration required, go to http://www27.compaq.com/SB/Exchange/Exchange2003/Index.asp). Dell has a tool named PowerMatch for Microsoft Exchange 2003 that can be downloaded from its website at http://www.dell.com/downloads/global/solutions/PMExchl.msi for offline use.

Network Operating System Requirements

When installing Exchange Server 2003, you have a server platform choice of Windows 2000 Server SP3 or later or Windows Server 2003. Although Exchange 2003 will operate just fine on Windows 2000, where possible, it is recommended that you install Exchange 2003 on a server running Windows Server 2003. Then you can take advantage of additional reliability and performance features available only with this server combination, such as the Volume Shadow Copy Service and the Windows Cluster Service with up to eight-node clustering capability. Other advantages of using Windows Server 2003 include a highly manageable release of IIS, Kerberos authentication, and IP Security (IPSec) for communication between front-end and back-end servers.

In addition to installing the correct version of the server software, you must make sure that certain core services components are installed and configured before initiating the installation of Exchange 2003. You can check whether they are installed in the services applet with the administrative tools on the Start menu. The core services components are as follows:

- Internet Information Services (IIS)

- Network News Transfer Protocol (NNTP) service

- Sample Mail Transfer Protocol (SMTP) service

- World Wide Web Publishing Service

The enabling of these components is handled differently, depending on the version of server software installed. When installing Exchange 2003 on a Windows 2003 Service Pack Three (SP3) server, you must install IIS, the World Wide Web Publishing service, the SMTP service, and the NNTP service manually before starting the Exchange installation.

Caution   The Exchange setup wizard checks for these components and will fail and error out if they are missing. If the components are installed, the Exchange wizard will continue and automatically install the ASP.NET and Microsoft .NET Framework.

If you are installing Exchange 2003 on a Windows Server 2003 server, none of these are installed; they are disabled by default. Each component must be installed manually before you start the Exchange Server 2003 setup program.

Tip   Be sure to review what services are enabled after the installation is completed. Servers that are being upgraded may retain previous service settings. For security reasons, disable services that are not being used, such as NNTP, POP3, IMAP, and so on. In new server installations, only the required default settings are enabled.

Features No Longer Supported

As expected, Microsoft wanted this version of Exchange to be the best product released to date. With the release of Exchange 2000, Microsoft had lost focus of what Exchange is supposed to be—a messaging platform. The introduction of collaboration and presence features in Exchange 2000 subtracted from the core goal of providing the best messaging platform and instead made the product among the front-runners but not the best. Exchange 2003 changed that and got back to the goal of being a great messaging platform. Let's examine the features that are no longer included in Exchange 2003.

Chat, Instant Messaging, Conferencing

In Exchange 2003, Microsoft removed the Microsoft Exchange Chat service, which was available in the Exchange 2000 Enterprise Edition. Unlike instant messaging (IM), which is an ad hoc environment, Exchange chat implemented virtual chat rooms that supported one-on-one communications and multiparty chats. Although Exchange Chat can still be used in mixed environments with Exchange 2000 and Exchange 2003, the feature must be removed before upgrading the entire server environment to Exchange 2003.

Microsoft also removed the Exchange Instant Messaging feature from Exchange 2003. Microsoft faced several issues in this arena with client compatibility, communication security, and incompatibility with other IM platforms such as Yahoo, MSN, and AOL. The inability to combine users of different systems—for example Exchange and Yahoo—into one conversation was a big shortcoming in leveraging the availability of presence information.

Microsoft also removed the Exchange Conferencing Server (ECS) from the feature set of Exchange 2003. An add-in product that ran on top of Exchange 2000, ECS provided audio, video, and data conferencing as well as conference-scheduling management. Because there is no replacement product for ECS in Exchange 2003, you'll need to look at Microsoft Office Live Meeting for ECS-type features.

Microsoft has not left the arena in regard to its collaboration and presence products. It has continued its efforts to develop stable, reliable, and functional products to fulfill customer needs for real-time communications. Microsoft Live Communications Server 2005 (MCLS 2005) delivers instant messaging (IM) and presence as part of a scalable, enterprise-caliber solution. MCLS 2005 offers enhanced security, seamless integration with other Microsoft products, and a development platform that can be enhanced by programmers. The product functionality is based on the Session Initiation Protocol (SIP) and SIP for Instant Messaging and Presence Leveraging Extensions (SIMPLE), as well as the Real Time Protocol (RTP). Check out this product if you require real-time communications in your organization.

M: Drive

Officially known as the Exchange Installable File System (ExIFS) in Exchange 2000, on new Exchange 2000 installations and upgrades from Exchange 5.5, ExIFS was automatically assigned to the M: drive and mapped to the information store as a way to programmatically manipulate items in the information store. To prevent unintentional data-corruption issues that may occur as a result of manually modifying data on drive M, or as a result of file-level virus scanning or backup-and-restore operations on drive M, Microsoft discontinued the drive mapping in Exchange 2003. If this mapping is required for legacy applications or mission-critical applications, you can enable the M: (or any other drive letter) back into the \\.\BackOfficeStorage\ namespace via a Registry key setting. However, the recommendation is to leave this feature disabled.

 Note   See instructions for enabling the M: drive in Exchange 2003 at Microsoft's website (http://support.microsoft.com) in Knowledge Base article 821836. Instructions for removing this feature in Exchange 2000 are located in Knowledge Base article 305145.

MAPI, MAPI Common Message Calls

Although Exchange 2003 is still a solid platform for development for application programming interfaces (APIs), data access methods, and other coding objects, some of the development technologies have been removed. Exchange 2003 no longer supports the use of Common Message Calls (CMC), which offers the basic capability to send and receive messages from messaging-aware applications, or Simple MAPI (SMAPI), which contains 12 Windows-based programming calls. Both of these features are interfaces to the Messaging Application Programming Interface (MAPI) subsystem, the heart of Microsoft's messaging programs. Even though these features have been removed, programmers can still develop applications via the Extended MAPI, which serves as the programming interface for C++ developers.

Legacy Connectors

As with the other deprecated features mentioned in the previous subsections, several mail connectors available in Exchange 2000 and earlier versions have been removed in Exchange 2003. These legacy connectors can exist in a mixed Exchange 2000/Exchange 2003 messaging environment, but must be removed prior to upgrading to Exchange 2003. The legacy connectors are as follows:

- Schedule Free/Busy Connector
- Directory Synchronization Connector
- Microsoft Exchange MS Mail Connector
- Microsoft Exchange Connector for Lotus cc:Mail

Summary

As you have read, Exchange Server 2003 is packed with new features designed to boost productivity levels for the end user and the administrators. Enhancements to the core messaging application provide improvements in the areas of administration, email access, security, and reliability, making Exchange 2003 the leader in the world of messaging platforms.

Those familiar with older versions of Exchange will welcome the new Exchange Deployment tools and the extensive preinstallation checklist that helps ensure a smooth installation of Exchange. After the installation process is completed, administrators will continue to benefit from the additions, changes, and advancements in tools, such as the updated Internet Mail Wizard, the Move Mailbox Wizard, the Message Recovery Center, and the improved Exchange System Manager.

LESSON 2

Understanding Exchange 2003 and Active Directory

The lesson covers the basic concepts of using Active Directory and exploring server architectures with Exchange Server 2003.

Why Active Directory?

Exchange Server 2003 relies heavily on the Microsoft Active Directory (AD) directory service for all its directory operations. Active Directory provides mailbox information, address lists information, and other recipient-related information. Active Directory also stores Exchange 2003 configuration information and acts as a security guard, ensuring that only authorized users can access mailboxes and only authorized administrators can modify the Exchange configuration in the organization.

Exchange 2003 also extends Active Directory to include a number of Exchange-specific attributes and classes by importing a series of .ldf files into Active Directory during the exchange setup process. A list of the .ldf files (Schema0.ldf to Schema9.ldf) are in the \Setup\i386\Exchange directory on the Exchange Server CD; Exschema.ldf is located in the \Setup\i386\Exchange\Bin directory. In addition to the schema changes, there are certain advantages that Active Directory brings to Exchange 2003.

Active Directory Advantages

Improvements in Active Directory deliver many key benefits for medium and large enterprises, enabling greater administrator and user productivity.

Windows Server 2003 improves the versatility, manageability, and dependability of the Active Directory found in previous server versions. While benefiting from lower cost and higher productivity, organizations will also benefit from the following:

- Easier deployment and management
- Improved performance
- Greater security

Deployment and management is significantly easier with improved migration and management tools, such as Active Directory Migration Tool (ADMT) 2.0 and the Domain Rename feature, which gives you the capability to rename Active Directory domains. Another tool, the Microsoft Group Policy Management Console (GPMC), provides a single solution for managing all Group Policy-related tasks for multiple domains and sites within a given forest using a simple user interface with drag-and-drop support.

Performance has been significantly improved; administrators now have more control over AD replication and synchronization between domain controllers in the same domain and across domains. The replication process has been improved within Active Directory so administrators can intelligently select only changed information for replication, no longer requiring updating entire portions of the directory over slow WAN links. In addition, the capability to log on with cached credentials without having to contact a global catalog server improves system performance for remote offices over slow or problematic WAN links.

As a result of Microsoft's Trustworthy Computing Initiative, security has also been improved within Active Directory. Cross-forests trust provides an easy way for managing security between two forests and simplifies cross-forest administration and authentication. Not only do administrators benefit, but users benefit from single sign-on (SSO) capability when accessing resources residing outside their own forest. A new addition to Active Directory, the Credential Manager provides a secure store of user credentials, passwords, and X.509 certificates. Because all this information is contained in a single place, the new Credential Manager provides a consistent SSO experience for users, no matter where they access their network.

Requirements for Exchange Server 2003

Exchange 2003 works with Active Directory similar to Exchange 2000 and benefits from the same preparations and planning as with Exchange 2000. Prior to Exchange 2000, Exchange could be installed only in a Windows NT domain. Because of its dependence on Active Directory, Exchange Server 2003 can be deployed only in Windows 2000 and Windows Server 2003 environments.

> **Caution**   Although Active Directory is a requirement for Exchange 2003, Exchange 2003 should not be installed on a domain controller because of security and performance issues.

A global catalog server, which holds information about users and mailboxes, is required in addition to Active Directory. The global catalog server must be at least Windows 2000 SP3 or later or Windows Server 2003 and must reside in each Active Directory site that contains an Exchange Server 2003.

The security boundary of Active Directory is called the *forest*. A one-to-one relationship exists between Active Directory forests and Exchange organizations; a forest can have only one Exchange organization, and an Exchange organization can span one forest but not multiple forests.

After preliminary Active Directory planning is complete, the directory must be extended to install Exchange. ForestPrep prepares Active Directory and extends the schema with additional object classes; the schema acts as the "governor," which enforces the rules and maintains the structure and content of Active Directory. To run ForestPrep, you must be logged in to the local machine with administrator rights and be a domain administrator. Similarly, you must be logged in to the domain as part of the Enterprise Admin and Schema Admin groups. After ForestPrep is completed, the domain must be prepped for Exchange 2003.

Tip It can take a considerable amount of time to update the schema via ForestPrep. When the schema update is finished, the new changes are replicated from the computer on which they were made to every other domain controller in the AD forest. Because this can have a negative effect on the network, depending on the number of domain controllers, it is recommended that you run this tool during off hours or when network activity is minimal.

Like ForestPrep, DomainPrep is run during the Exchange installation process (or as a standalone process) and must be run in each domain that supports Exchange users or Exchange 2003 servers. DomainPrep prepares the domain for Exchange 2003 by creating security groups, containers, and setting permissions necessary for Exchange 2003. To run DomainPrep, you must be logged in to the local machine with administrator rights. Similarly, you must be logged in to the domain as a Domain Admin. After DomainPrep is completed, the Exchange 2003 installation process can continue.

Why Windows Server 2003?

With multiprocessor support for 8-way Pentium and XEON processors, memory-tuning options via the /3GB switch and /USERVA switch, and IPSec server communication between Exchange 2003 front-end and back-end servers, Windows Server 2003 is the operating system of choice. Although Exchange Server 2003 can be run on Windows 2000 Server SP3 and later, Windows Server 2003 should be run to take advantage of enterprise class features, such as enhanced reliability, remote access, and server clustering.

Server Reliability

Windows Server 2003 improves on the server platform reliability delivered in Windows 2000 Server. With improvements in the underlying server architecture, Active Directory performance, management, and maintenance tools, as well as support for new technologies such as the Volume Shadow Copy Service (VSS) and server clustering, Windows Server 2003 represents major enhancements to the reliability and scalability of Exchange 2003. Cluster Fail Over and Fail Back technology and snapshot backup technology with VSS will dramatically reduce server downtime and provide creative options for disaster recovery. Because the reliability of the server platform has been significantly improved, organizations can look at reducing costs by reducing the amount of money spent on purchasing and supporting multiple servers and network infrastructure.

 Tip   Most vendors of backup products have updated their software to support VSS. Make sure your backup product supports this feature so that you can take advantage of new and creative ways to back up and restore your Exchange mailboxes and server data quickly and efficiently.

Remote Access

Windows Server 2003 also significantly improves remote access capability for Exchange users. One of the most noted improvements is the capability for Outlook 2003 users to communicate securely with Exchange servers via RPC over an HTTP connection. This connection over the Internet eliminates the need for tunneling technologies such as Virtual Private Networks (VPNs), smart cards, and other secure access technologies. Coupled with the new Outlook 2003 Cached mode, which allows users to have a full copy of their mailboxes available at all times and eliminates the need for a continuous connection to the email server or network, RPC over HTTP provides a secure and reliable method for remote access across slow or problematic network connections. This option is available only with Windows 2003 Server.

Server Clustering

Clustering services in Windows Server 2003 provide dramatic improvements by enhancing existing features found in previous versions and also offering new key options. Unlike Windows 2000 Server cluster support for only two nodes, Windows Server 2003 Enterprise Edition and Datacenter Edition provide support for up to 8-node clustering. Clusters can be created in various active/passive node configurations, such as seven active/one passive or four active/four passive or in an Active/Passive with as little as one Passive node.

Note   Active/Active is only supported in 2-node clusters and is limited to only 1,900 concurrent connections and an average CPU utilization of 40% or less. If these restrictions cannot be met, additional Exchange servers or Exchange Virtual Servers will be needed.

With preconfigurations, remote administration, and default settings, installation and setup are easier and more robust; basic server clusters can be up and running quickly, and with fewer server reboots.

Clustering services are also closely integrated with Active Directory. This tight integration includes features such as Kerberos authentication, delegation, and security, and Active Directory-aware service integration with other services that publish information to Active Directory.

Enhanced network features such as improved failover logic, media sense detection, and multicast heartbeats provide greater failover capabilities and high system uptime. In addition, all internal cluster communications are signed and secure. With the addition of real-time monitoring tools, such as ClusDiag and ClusterRecovery, support personnel can locate failures and possible future cluster problems.

Understanding Front-End Servers

Front-end servers are deployed in an Exchange Server architecture that distributes server tasks among front-end and back-end servers. In this architecture, a front-end server accepts requests from clients and proxies them to the appropriate back-end server for processing and management of the information store. Exchange Server 2003 enhances the front-end and back-end server architecture of Exchange 2000 and adds new features and capabilities, such as RPC over HTTP communication, that enables users with Outlook 2003 clients to access their Exchange information from the Internet. In addition, the HTTP communication between front-end and back-end servers is enabled with Kerberos authentication by default; no longer is it necessary to configure and enable IPSec server-to-server communication unless the server is in a public network. Moreover, the scalability of the exchange organization is now enhanced because the topology can grow as the organization grows; back-end servers can easily be added to handle additional users, connections, or processing requests. Finally, the standard version of Exchange Server 2003 can also be configured as a front-end server, reducing initial software costs.

Using front-end and back-end server technology also provides the following advantages both for remote users accessing email over the Internet and users who are located on the internal network:

- Single Namespace—A single, consistent namespace such as https://Outlook Web Access Server/exchange for mailbox access allows administrative flexibility when adding or removing back-end servers, without affecting users who are accessing the front-end server. A single namespace also remains scalable for HTTP, POP, or IMAP access as the organization grows and reduces the number of server SSL certificates, because client computers are using SSL to the same servers and namespace.

- Offloading of SSL encryption and decryption—SSL traffic presents a large overhead for Exchange servers. In a front-end and back-end setup, the front-end server assumes the load of the SSL encryption, freeing up the back-end server to handle email requests and processing only, improving overall email performance for the users.

- Improved Public Folder access—Because a front-end server knows the state of a back-end server, the front-end server can provide multiple requests to public folder data and system data, such as calendar free/busy information. Exchange 2003 enhances the usability of OWA when using a front-end server by allowing OWA users to read, reply, and forward public folder postings.

Public folder posts can be read only in a non–front-end server topology.

- Security—The front-end server can be positioned as the single point of access in front of or behind a firewall. It contains no user data stored in the server and acts as an additional layer of security for the exchange organization against Denial of Service attacks, authenticating requests before proxying them to the back-end servers. Any services that are not needed can be disabled on these servers for further security hardening.

Note   These are just a few of the advantages provided by a front-end/back-end server architecture. To fully understand the advantages of this architecture, check out whitepapers available on the Microsoft Exchange website at http://www.microsoft.com/exchange/default.mspx.

Typical Scenarios for Front-End Servers

There are common implementation scenarios for front-end and back-end server architecture. The first implementation involves email clients (Outlook, POP, or IMAP, OWA [HTTP], OMA [HTTP]) and a network or Internet connection to the front-end server that is serving requests to the back-end server over the internal network. As shown in Figure 2.1 and 2.2, this configuration involves limited security with the front-end server acting as a single layer of protection between the network or Internet and the back-end Exchange server.

The second scenario, shown in Figure 2.3, involves more security that includes an advanced firewall, such as Microsoft's Internet Security and Acceleration (ISA) service configured with Service Pack 1 and the latest feature packs. The advanced firewall is located between the network or Internet and the front-end server.

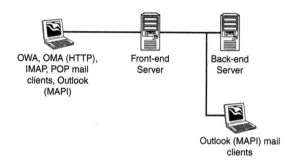

FIGURE 2.1   Basic front-end and back-end server architecture with network connection and no firewall.

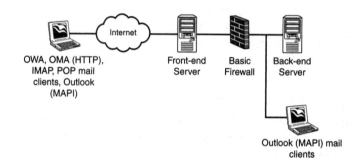

FIGURE 2.2   Basic front-end and back-end server architecture with Internet connection and no firewall.

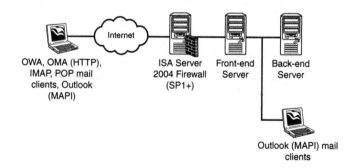

FIGURE 2.3   The recommended front-end and back-end server architecture with advanced firewall configuration.

This configuration provides greater security and limits the front-end server's exposure to unwanted intruders. The firewall becomes the focal point for Denial of Service attacks and intrusion/penetration attacks rather than the front-end server. This scenario represents the recommended configuration for front-end and back-end server architecture.

Understanding Back-End Servers

Back-end servers are the servers that do most of the work in an Exchange front-end and back-end server topology. All the email service requests are forwarded from the front-end servers to back-end servers, which are considered the workhorses of the Exchange architecture. Because there can be multiple servers in a front-end and back-end architecture, load balancing can be configured to spread the access requests across all the servers. Splitting the client requests among several back-end servers optimizes messaging performance and provides a scalable server architecture.

Typical Scenarios for Back-End Servers

As the workhorses of the Exchange organization, back-end servers can be configured as a single server or a farm of multiple servers serving a front-end server or servers.

The basic architecture looks like Figure 2.4. As you can see, the figure contains email clients, a front-end server to proxy requests, and a back-end server to process the requests and store the Exchange information.

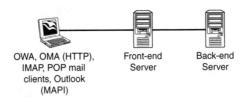

OWA, OMA (HTTP),   Front-end   Back-end
IMAP, POP mail   Server   Server
clients, Outlook
(MAPI)

FIGURE 2.4   Basic placement of back-end servers.

An advanced architecture shown in Figure 2.5 includes a firewall in addition to the front-end server to enhance the network and server environment and help prevent unwanted persons from accessing the server directly. In this scenario, the firewall and the front-end server are the focal points for intruders, not the back-end server where sensitive user and organization data is held.

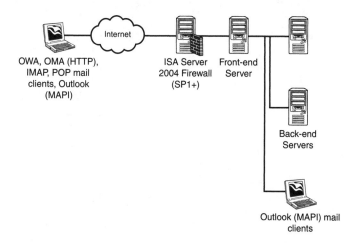

FIGURE 2.5   Advanced placement of back-end servers.

As shown in Figure 2.6, another scenario exists where there are multiple networked mail servers located behind the front-end server, also known as a server farm. A back-end server farm streamlines internal processes by distributing the workload between the individual servers of the farm using network load-balancing technology and expedites computing processes by harnessing the power of multiple servers. The load-balancing software tracks demand for processing power from different computers, prioritizing the tasks, and scheduling and rescheduling them depending on network user priority and demand. When one server in the farm fails, another can step in as a backup.

These are just a few of the configurations that can be architected in an Exchange deployment. Make sure that you research and deploy the configuration that best fits your organization.

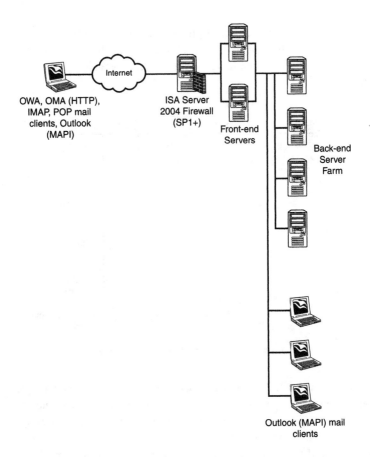

FIGURE 2.6   Front-end and back-end architecture with a back-end server farm.

Summary

Exchange Server 2003 relies heavily on the Microsoft Active Directory (AD) directory service for all its directory operations. Active Directory acts as a provider of information (mailbox, recipient, or address lists) and as a security guard to this information so that only authorized users and administrators have access. Coupled with new features found in Windows

Server 2003, such as memory tuning, Volume Shadow Copy Service, remote access, and clustering, Exchange 2003 has increased performance and reliability necessary for the enterprise. A front-end and back-end server architecture adds additional scalability and reliability to a messaging environment. Whereas the front-end server provides an extra layer of security and handles SSL duties, the back-end server benefits users with an increased capability to process client requests and to load balance requests across a back-end server farm.

LESSON 3

Managing Users, Contacts, and Groups

This lesson explores managing users, contacts, and groups in Exchange Server 2003.

Administering Active Directory

In an Exchange organization, administrators spend a great deal of time dealing with users, contacts, and groups. The Exchange 2003 administration tools are very similar to those of Exchange 2000 and require very little additional training to get started. New features include drag-and-drop capability, an enhanced interface, and updated versions of the administration tools.

Although the tools and features have been updated since Exchange 2000, working with Exchange 2003 administration tools is easier for experienced administrators. The new tools are easier to use and time-saving as well for repetitive administration tasks. Overworked and underfunded administrators will rejoice with the newfound set of tools and productivity!

To manage Windows 2003 and some of the features of Exchange 2003, it is recommended that you install the administration tools on a workstation running Windows XP with Service Pack 1 or later. Using your server as the administration console exposes the server to unwanted risks, such as accidentally deleting system files or inadvertently introducing viruses. Be sure to have your Windows 2003 CD available because it will be needed to install the admin tools. (If the CD is not available, the appropriate version can be downloaded online from Microsoft.) For a successful workstation installation, use the following checklist:

- Install Microsoft Windows XP Professional SP1 or later.

- Join the workstation to the domain with Exchange 2003.

- Install the Windows Server 2003 Administration Tools Pack.

- Install the Simple Mail Transfer Protocol service (SMTPSVC).

- Install the Exchange System Management Tools.

- Shut down the SMTPSVC service (for security reasons).

To install the administration tools, locate the administration pack file, adminpak.msi, which is on the Windows Server 2003 CD in the \i386 directory, and then double-click the file. This will install all the tools available for administering Windows 2003. After the installation is complete, the tools can be accessed through the Administration Tools group on the Start menu. Remember that to work with these tools, the user must be logged on to the domain with administrative privileges in the domain.

 Tip Active Directory User and Computers (ADUC) is one tool that is used frequently by administrators. To minimize the amount of mouse clicking and provide quick access to ADUC, pin a shortcut to the program on the Start menu.

Exchange-specific tasks are accomplished with the Exchange administration tools found on the Exchange 2003 CD. To use these tools, the IIS Snap-in, the World Wide Web Publishing Service, the Windows Server 2003 Administration Tools, and the SMTP Service must be available on your workstation. Look in Control Panel, Add/Remove Programs, Add/Remove Windows Components, then double-click Internet Information Services to check whether the components are installed; if not, check the option to install. The components are required to run the setup program on the Exchange 2003 CD. When you're prompted for the type of installation, choose Custom and select the option to install the Exchange System Management tools. After this is completed, the Start menu will contain an Exchange System Management group with the Exchange specific toolset.

Caution   Remember that to manage Exchange 2003, the management workstation must be part of the same forest as your Exchange servers. The workstation cannot manage domains in a different forest.

Managing Users with Active Directory

Although the Exchange Task Wizard can also be used to create, delete, and move mailboxes, Active Directory Users and Computers (ADUC) is the tool primarily used by Exchange administrators for managing users and contacts. This tool creates mailboxes and mail-enabled users and manages directory contacts and mail-enabled contacts. ADUC is also good for looking at user properties, such as contact info, Exchange alias, or server info. The Exchange Task Wizard is useful for creating a mailbox on a user account that was created without a mailbox. Be sure to install the ESM toolkit on the administration workstation; otherwise, the Exchange Feature tab and context menus will not be available in ADUC.

Note   After Exchange 2003 has been installed and appears to be in working order, the installation must be validated with some simple testing. The testing process involves setting up a test user to validate that email can be sent to and received from the server, that mail flow occurs between servers, and that OWA functions as expected.

Mailbox administration of Exchange users is accomplished though the ADUC tool. To create a mailbox, complete the following steps:

1. Click Start, All Programs, Microsoft Exchange, Active Directory Users and Computers.

2. Expand the domain, click Users, and right-click the Active Directory user account for which you want to create a mailbox. Select All Tasks, and then select Exchange Tasks.

3. Click Next to bypass the Exchange Tasks Welcome page. To prevent future displays of the Welcome page, click the Do Not Show This Welcome Page again check box.

4. Confirm that the Create Mailbox option is highlighted and then click Next.

5. Type in an alias name for the user, the server name, and the mailbox store name, as shown in Figure 3.1. If you're unsure of the correct alias, server, or mailbox store to use, accept the default values and then click Next to continue. Click Finish to complete the wizard.

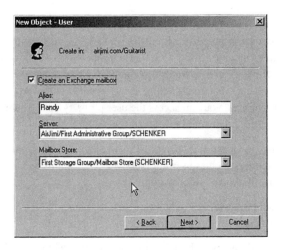

FIGURE 3.1   Configuring the Exchange mailbox options.

After the user is enabled, use Outlook Web Access to test the mail functionality. This is an easy way to make sure that the mail-enabled user can send and receive email through the Exchange Server. This also confirms that web services are working properly, that the server architecture (front-end and back-end servers) is communicating properly, and that the OWA traffic is delivered through the organization's firewall. The test can be completed using the following steps:

1. Open Internet Explorer and browse to http://{servername}/ exchange.

2. Log in to the Exchange server with the newly created Exchange user's credentials and then send email to an existing Exchange user.

3. With a second instance of Internet Explorer, log in as the existing Exchange user, confirm receipt of the email from the new Exchange user, and then send a reply back to the new Exchange user.

4. Confirm that email messages were sent and received from both accounts.

The Exchange Task Wizard is useful for basic configuration and setup, but the majority of user property administrative tasks are still performed within Active Directory using ADUC. The property tabs associated with an Active Directory user account contain information related to both the user and Exchange. By right-clicking a user account within ADUC and selecting Properties, you can access the user property tabs. There are four Exchange-specific tabs of interest to administrators:

- Exchange General Exchange—Provides access to general mailbox settings such as user alias, delivery restrictions and options, and mailbox store information.

- Exchange Advanced—Shows the display name, the address list, and custom settings for attributes and mailbox rights.

- Email Addresses—Used for creating and maintaining multiple email addresses associated with a single user.

- Exchange Features—For enabling or disabling wireless service settings (OMA, user synchronization and notification) and protocol options (IMAP4, POP4, or OWA) for email access.

Most of these setting are initially configured with default global settings; on these pages, you make individual user changes and settings. For example, an administrator can change a user property for the OMA feature by following these steps:

1. Right-click a user in Active Directory Users and Computers and select Properties. Then select the Exchange Features tab.

2. Select the Outlook Mobile Access option and click enable or disable as necessary to change the status. (To change the properties of a protocol, select the protocol and then click Properties.)

3. Click OK to finish.

Exchange Task Wizard is helpful for enabling user accounts that were not created with a mailbox. Because it is not required to create a mailbox when a user is created, the Exchange Task Wizard is useful for basic configuration and setting up a user to send and receive email messages. Using the following steps, a mailbox can be added to a user account:

1. In Active Directory Users and Computers, right-click a user's name and select Exchange Tasks to initiate the Exchange Task Wizard.

2. Click Next at the Welcome page.

3. Under Available Tasks, select the option Create Mailbox and then click Next. The Create Mailbox Wizard dialog box is displayed.

4. By default, the Exchange alias is set to the logon name. This option is changed by entering a new alias name.

Note The Exchange alias can be changed only if a single user account is having a mailbox added. If multiple user accounts are selected, the Exchange alias will be set to the user's logon name and cannot be changed as described in step 4.

5. If multiple Exchange servers are configured with an Information Store, or if multiple mailbox stores have been configured, use the relevant drop-down list to specify the proper server or mailbox store that should be used.

6. Click Next and then click Finish to complete the mailbox addition to the user account.

Managing Contacts

Contacts in Exchange 2003 represent people inside and outside the organization who users want to communicate with. Contacts can have directory information associated with them, but not have network logon privileges. The two types of contacts are standard contacts and mail-enabled contacts. Unlike standard contacts, which have no associated email addresses, mail-enabled contacts have one or more associated email addresses. Contacts with email addresses can be listed in the Global Address List (GAL) or other address lists in an organization, allowing others to send messages to them.

Creating a standard or a mail-enabled contact is accomplished fairly easily using the following steps:

1. Click Start, All Programs, Microsoft Exchange, Active Directory Users and Computers.

2. Right-click in the container to hold the new contact, select New, and then select Contact. The New Object-Contact dialog box will open as shown in Figure 3.2.

3. Complete the form fields for first name, initial, and last name. The full name that is displayed in Active Directory User and Computers is filled in automatically. The full name is also used by other users when searching the directory for a contact.

4. If the contact requires a name that is different from the full name, fill in the display name field. The display name is shown in the GAL and other organization address lists and is used when addressing emails to the contact. Click Next to continue.

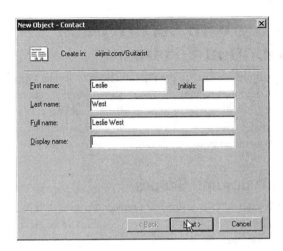

FIGURE 3.2 Entering new contact information.

5. If a mail-enabled contact is not required, uncheck the Create an Exchange E-Mail address option and skip directly to step 7.

6. Fill in the Exchange alias for the contact and click the Modify button. A dialog box for entering the email address appears. Select the type of email address required by the organization, such as SMTP, and then click OK. In the next dialog box, complete the properties for the contact and then click OK.

7. Click Next and then click Finish, creating the new contact.

Additional information can also be set for a contact by opening the properties page for a contact. Double-click the contact's name in ADUC to see the options available for modification. Each property tab contains different contact info that can be modified. The General tab contains general contact information such as the contact's name, office location, or primary telephone number. The Address tab provides fields for the contact's business address. The Telephones tab contains options for adding multiple additional telephone numbers. The Organization tab contains settings for the contact's title, department, and company name. After the modifications are completed, be sure to click Apply or OK to apply and set the changes.

Working with Security and Distribution Groups

In general, groups are used to grant permissions to similar types of users, to make contact of multiple users easier, and to simplify administration. For example, instead of having to enter 10 email addresses in the message header, a message can be sent to one group email, which is then fanned out to all 10 email addresses in the group.

Group Types and Scopes

Microsoft Windows 2003 defines different group types, with each group having a unique scope. The three group types that can be created within Active Directory are

- Security Groups—Groups used to secure access to network resources via permissions; they can also be used to distribute email messages.

- Distribution Groups—Groups that can be used only to distribute email; they have a fixed membership that can't be used to access network resources.

- Query-Based Distribution Groups (QBDGs)—These groups are new to Exchange 2003. Their membership is based on a LDAP (Lightweight Distribution Access Protocol) query that can be used only to distribute email. Using LDAP, a member list is created whenever messages are sent to a group.

So what is the main difference between a security and a distribution group? Although both groups can have an email address associated with them, a distribution group cannot be used to set security settings. For example, you cannot create a distribution group called Project Team and then assign security rights to that group.

When you are working with distribution and security groups, there are many things that can or cannot be done, depending on the group's scope and the mode that Windows Server is running. The are three types of scopes—global, domain local, and universal—and two type of modes, mixed or native. See Table 3.1 for a summary of what can and cannot be done according to the network operating mode.

TABLE 3.1 Understanding Group Scope, Group Membership, and Windows Operating Mode

Scope	Group Membership	Windows Mixed Mode	Windows Native Mode
Domain Local	Permission assigned only in the same domain; can be put into other domain local groups.	Global groups and accounts from any domain.	Global groups, accounts, and universal groups from any domain. Domain local groups can be only from the same domain.
Global	Permissions assigned in any domain; can be put into other groups.	Can contain accounts only from the same domain.	Global groups and accounts only from the same domain.
Universal	Can be assigned permissions in any domain and can be put into other groups.	Not available in mixed mode domains.	Regardless of scope, can contain accounts or groups from any domain.

Creating Security or Distribution Groups

Using the following steps, administrators can create security or distribution groups:

1. Open Active Directory User and Computers. Right-click in the container where you want to create a new group, select New, and then select Group.

2. As shown in Figure 3.3, the New Object-Group dialog box will appear. In the Group Name field, type up to a 64 character name for the new group. The first 20 characters will be automatically inserted for the Pre-Windows 2000 group name and must be unique for the domain. If needed, you can type a unique name into this field.

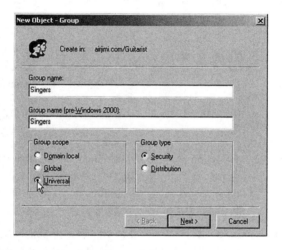

FIGURE 3.3 Creating security and distribution groups through Active Directory Users and Computers.

3. Select a group type of either Domain local, global, or universal (available only in native mode). The recommended scope type is universal; if you are unsure about which scope to use, choose universal.

4. Select Security or Distribution for your group type and click Next.

5. If the Exchange is set up properly, the Create an Exchange Email Address option will be available. Make sure that the box is checked and that the correct Alias name for the email address is displayed. (By default, the alias name is set to the group name.) If an Exchange email address isn't needed, uncheck this option.

6. Click Next and then click Finish, creating the group. If creation of an email address was selected, SMTP and X.400 email addresses will be automatically created.

After the group is created, administrators can change additional group properties, such as adding members to the group, setting message size-restriction limits, adding or removing email addresses, or limiting which users can send messages to the group.

Creating Query-Based Distribution Groups

Query-based distribution groups do not have a scope that is domain local, global, or universal. Their membership can contain users and groups from other domains or forests or members of the local domain. Their scope is determined by the container associated with the group when it is created. For example, if the container associated with the group is pandoranet-works.com, the query filter is applied to all recipients in the domain. If a filter is applied to a specific organization unit (OU) in a domain, the filter applies to all recipients in the container and those in any containers below.

 Note   Query-based distribution groups are available only when Exchange is running in native mode and all servers in the enterprise are at least running Exchange 2000 SP3 or later. An administrator can check which mode Exchange is in by opening ESM, clicking the Exchange Organization, and then selecting Properties. Review the Operation Mode section to see what mode your Exchange server is currently running in.

The beauty of query-based distribution groups is that less time is spent managing group membership. In most organizations, people move around the company to different roles, departments, or eventually leave the company. Instead of specifying static user memberships, query-based distribution groups minimize the amount of time spent adding or removing users from groups by allowing LDAP queries to dynamically build membership in the distribution group. The group membership is created on-the-fly. An LDAP query is run every time an email is sent to this dynamic distribution list. Thus, using query-based distribution groups can dramatically reduce the administrative costs.

Caution   Query-based distribution groups work best when the member list results are 25 to 30 members or fewer. Potential member lists in the hundreds or thousands will put severe processing demands on a global catalog server because of the inefficient nature of the LDAP queries. If query-based distribution groups have potential to grow to larger numbers, switching the processing tasks from the global catalog server to a dedicated LDAP expansion server will help in resolving large distribution lists more quickly.

Because groups are used to manage email distribution and permissions, remember to create groups that will contain similar types of users. Typically, administrators create groups for users who work in the same departments and need access to similar network resources, users who have similar roles in an organization (executives, directors, engineers, and so on), or for users on specific company projects. Using the following steps, administrators can create query-based distribution groups:

1. Open Active Directory User and Computers. Right-click in the container where you want to create a new group, select New, and then select Query-Based Distribution Group.

2. As shown in Figure 3.4, the New Object-Query-based Distribution Group dialog box will appear. Type in a group name and, if required, a different alias for the group. Otherwise, the group name will be automatically inserted for the Exchange alias and will be used to set the group email address.

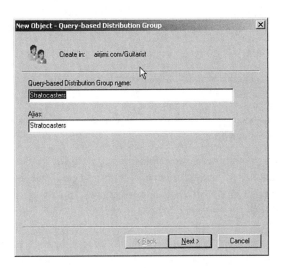

FIGURE 3.4   Creating query-based distribution groups through Active Directory Users and Computers.

3. The container in which the group is created defines the scope of the LDAP query. This means the query filter will apply to all recipients of the container selected and below the specified container. Choose one of the preconfigured filters; otherwise, select the Customize Filter option and click Customize. The Find Exchange Recipients dialog box, as shown in Figure 3.5, appears.

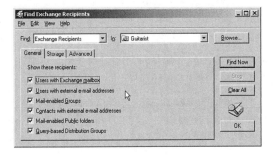

FIGURE 3.5   Customizing the LDAP query filter parameters in the Find Exchange Recipients dialog box.

4. Use the following tabs to configure additional parameters:

- General—Used to select the recipient types in the group.

- Storage—Used to limit the mailbox to a specific server or mailbox store.

- Advanced—Used to create combinations of fields, operators, and search criteria.

5. When you're finished selecting criteria, click OK to return to the wizard. Click Next and then click Finish to create the group. As with other groups, if creation of an email address was selected, SMTP and X.400 email addresses will be automatically created.

Again, after the group is created, administrators can manage additional group properties, such as adding members to the group, setting message size-restriction limits, changing, adding, or removing email addresses, limiting which users can send messages to the group, adding an expansion server, or configuring out-of-office options and nondelivery settings. Many settings can be configured; explore the ones that best fit your organization.

Renaming and Deleting Groups

Renaming and deleting groups each has a different effect on the security identifier (SID); object values are used to identify, handle, and track permissions independently of group names. When a group is renamed, the group is given a new label. Changing the name does not affect the SID, Exchange alias, or email addresses associates with the group. The group can be renamed in ADUC in two easy steps:

1. Right-click the group name and then select Rename. Type in the new group name and press Enter.

2. When the Rename Group dialog box appears, press Tab and type in a new pre-Windows 2000 group name; then click OK to complete the group rename.

Deleting a group removes it permanently from Active Directory. In theory, after a group is deleted, a group with the same name cannot be created with the same permissions of the original group. Group names can be reused, but because the SID of the new group name will not match the SID of the original group name, the permission settings must be manually re-created. Deleting a group is accomplished by highlighting the appropriate group, right-clicking, and selecting Delete or pressing the Delete key.

 Note   Windows has built-in security features that will not allow deletion of built-in groups. There is no right-click Delete option and pressing Delete yields no results. Other group types can be removed using the previous steps.

Summary

In an Exchange organization, administrators spend a great deal of time dealing with users, contacts, and groups. The administration tools are very similar to those of Exchange 2000 and require very little additional training to get started. The administration tools include new features, such as drag-and-drop capability, an enhanced interface, and updated versions of the administration tools. Although Active Directory Users and Computers is used for the majority of administrative tasks in Exchange 2003, the Exchange Task Wizard is also useful for basic configuration, setup, and administration on Exchange mailboxes, such as deleting, moving, and merging. Query-based distribution groups use LDAP queries to minimize group additions, deletions, and changes that normally absorb a lot of time for administrators.

LESSON 4

Managing Exchange Server 2003 via Exchange System Manager

This lesson explores various ways to manage Exchange Server 2003 using the Exchange System Manager.

What Is Exchange System Manager (ESM)?

Exchange System Manager (ESM) was first introduced with Exchange 2000 as a replacement for the Exchange Administrator used in previous versions of Exchange. Exchange System Manager is a specialized, preconfigured Microsoft Management Console (MMC), Exchange System Manager.msc, which helps you manage your Exchange organization. This file is located in the \Program Files\Exchsrvr\Bin directory. Unlike Exchange Administrator, ESM is an integrated toolbox that can be run along with other tools (Active Directory Users and Computers, Internet Services Manager, Event Viewer, and so on) in the same console, using context menus, by right-clicking with a mouse. When administrators perform a typical installation of Exchange 2003 onto a server, the installation wizard installs the Exchange System Management Tools onto that server by default. If the tools installed are not selected during setup, they are not installed during the Exchange Server software installation.

As Figure 4.1 shows, Exchange System Manager provides a GUI with a two-pane view of Exchange objects, with a console tree on the left and a details pane on the right. Administrators can manipulate some objects using a drag-and-drop operation. The ESM tool allows configuration of server settings, such as the following:

- Global Settings for all Exchange servers in the organization

- Address lists, templates, and policies for recipients

- Mailbox store, public folder, and server system policies

- Connectors for Novell GroupWise and Lotus Notes

- Message tracking, monitoring, and site replication

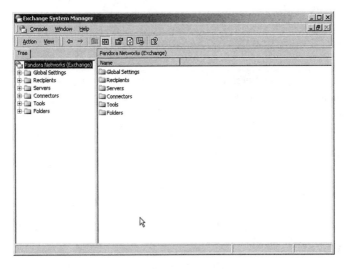

FIGURE 4.1   The Exchange System Manager main screen.

The preceding list is not complete; many more settings are available for configuration. As in an integrated toolbox, Exchange System Manager provides a consistent administrative interface for administrators who deal with all areas of Exchange server management, including policies, public folders, servers, and routing.

System Manager is available in the Microsoft Exchange Program group on the Start menu. You can view context menus for each object by right-clicking the object.

Installing the ESM

ESM is installed by using the Exchange setup program, which is called the Exchange System Management Tools. ESM is included as a part of the Typical installation type in Setup and can also be installed through the Custom installation type in Setup. Although the Exchange System Management Tools have been installed on the server itself, the management tools can be installed on any computer that is a member of the domain and that meets the minimum requirements as set by Microsoft and shown in Table 4.1.

TABLE 4.1—Understanding Minimum System Requirements for Exchange System Manager

Operating System	Version Supported	Service Packs	Additional Services
Windows XP	XP Professional	SP1 and later	Windows Server 2003 Administration Tools and IIS snap-in with WWW Publishing and SMTP services
Windows Server 2003	Standard, Enterprise, or Datacenter. The Web Edition is not supported		IIS management snap-in
Windows 2000	Server	SP3 or later	Windows 2000 Administration Tools and the SMTP and NNTP services

Operating System	Version Supported	Service Packs	Additional Services
Windows 2000	Professional	SP3 or later	Windows 2000 Administration Tools and the IIS management snap-in

On the Exchange Server, Exchange System Manager (ESM) is found by clicking Start, All Programs, and selecting the Microsoft Exchange program group. You will see the option for Exchange System Manager. Click this menu item to launch Exchange System Manager.

As recommended in Lesson 2, administrators are strongly encouraged to install the tools on a dedicated management workstation to reduce the possibility of introducing unwanted items to the server, such as viruses or Trojans. Following the interactive installation process, the basic steps are shown next:

1. When the Exchange 2003 CD (Standard or Enterprise) is inserted in the CD drive, the autorun feature displays a splash screen with the options Resources and Deployment Tools. Click Exchange Deployment Tools to initiate the installation.

2. On the Deployment Tools welcome screen, click Install Exchange System Management Tools Only. Review and confirm that preinstallation requirements are met and then click Run Setup Now.

3. Click Next and review the licensing agreement information. Select I Agree and then click Next to continue.

4. As shown in Figure 4.2, confirm that the Exchange Management Tools option is selected on the Component Selection page.

5. Click Next to continue the installation, and then click Finish when the installation is complete.

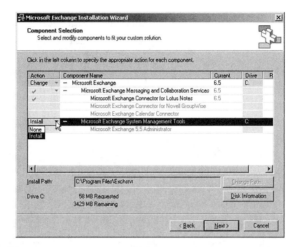

FIGURE 4.2 Installing the Exchange System Management Tools using the Exchange Server Installation Wizard.

Caution   For successful installation on certain platforms, the installation of ESM requires enabling extra services such as NNTP and WWW Publishing. For security reasons, be sure to disable any extra services if they are not needed for other applications.

Administrators may receive error messages if ESM is installed on systems that also run Microsoft Outlook. The error message warns that a recently installed program may cause Microsoft Office or other email-enabled programs to function improperly and asks to let Outlook resolve the problem. If Yes is selected, the system makes changes to MAPI core files and the system may need to be rebooted; most likely the error message will go away (yet this doesn't ensure that the problem goes away). If No is clicked, no changes are made to the core MAPI files. More information is available at the Microsoft support site, http://support.microsoft.com/. Search for Knowledge Base article 820865.

Tip Correcting the MAPI core files may or may not fix errors and stop error messages from appearing. Avoid MAPI error messages by accessing email messages using a Terminal Server session or Microsoft Outlook Web Access.

Backward Compatibility with ESM

Exchange System Manager is an MMC-based tool that provides administrators with a graphical user interface for managing the configuration of Exchange 2000 Server or Exchange Server 2003 organizations. Administrators of Exchange 2000 and earlier versions will be able to take advantage of Exchange 2003 ESM as soon as the first Exchange 2003 server is added to their organization. The caveat is that the administrators must run the ForestPrep procedure before using the Exchange 2003 ESM or when using the tool in a non-Microsoft supported environment.

Using ESM 2003 in mixed mode environments is supported; however, certain restrictions and limitations exist. As you know, Exchange System Manager 2003 can manage Exchange 2003, Exchange 2000, and Exchange 5.5 servers. Exchange System Manager 2003 cannot manage any components that existed in Exchange 2000 but that were removed from Exchange 2003, such as Key Management Service, Instant Messaging and Chat, or legacy connectors. Because these components are not supported, they will not appear in the ESM console. New Exchange features such as Queue Viewer, Move Mailbox, Mailbox Recovery Center, and Internet Mail Wizard can all be used in Exchange 2000 and Exchange 2003 environments.

There are a few things that administrators should remember:

- Do not use ESM in Exchange 2000 to manage or edit any Exchange 2003 server components. The Exchange 2000 ESM does not understand new objects in Exchange 2003, such as Outlook Mobile Access, and will cause damage and/or corruptions of the objects.

- Exchange ESM 2000 is not version aware. If you must manage Exchange 2000 and 2003 systems, be sure to install Exchange 2000 SP3 and the latest version of the SP3 Rollup patch. The combination of patches makes Exchange 2000 ESM version aware, preventing edits of objects requiring a later version of Exchange System Manager. A dialog error box will pop up on screen when this condition is met.

- Exchange 2000 ESM cannot be installed on an Exchange 2003 system, and vice versa.

- Exchange 2000 ESM and Exchange 2003 ESM cannot be installed on the same computer. If mixed mode operation is required in the organization, individual workstations will be required for each version of ESM.

 Tip   A simple workaround exists for managing a mixed-mode environment: use remote management access methods such as a Terminal Server session or Remote Desktop Services. This will keep the number of management workstations to a minimum.

Creating Mailbox Data Stores

Exchange 2003 uses two types of data stores as containers for information: mailbox stores, which store a server's mailboxes, and public stores, which store the server's public folders. Mailbox stores contain information about Exchange logons and mailbox usage. Public folder stores, discussed in the next section of this lesson, contain information about Exchange logons, replication, and public folder instances. Both stores contain information about full text indexing.

A default mailbox store is created in every Exchange organization. As an organization grows, additional mailbox stores can be created. In addition to accommodating more users in an organization, additional mailbox stores help with database recovery due to a failure, can improve Exchange performance by placing mailbox stores on different drives, and help with administration by allowing different sets of rules to be applied to different sets of users for items such as maintenance, security, or policies.

Creating a new mailbox store requires basic information: the name of the new mailbox store, where the store's database files will reside, a schedule for maintenance, mailbox size limits, and which default public folder to use.

To create a new mailbox store with ESM, use the following steps:

1. Select the Exchange server to manage. Right-click the necessary storage group, select New, and then click Mailbox Store.

2. As shown in Figure 4.3, the Properties dialog box appears. On the General tab, type the name of the mailbox store into the Name field. If changes to the default options are needed, change them here. Otherwise, default settings are okay.

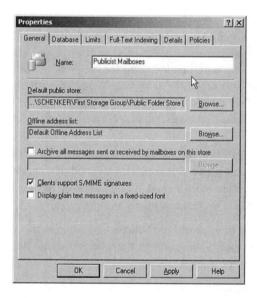

FIGURE 4.3   The Properties dialog box containing tabs for setting messaging properties.

3. Click the Database tab. If changes to the default database location are needed, change them here. The maintenance schedule can also be changed on this page by clicking the Customize button and setting a new time.

4. Click the Limits tab. The page contains options for the storage limits and deleted item retention for individual mailboxes and entire mailbox stores. Configure settings in accordance with organizational storage policies and procedures.

5. Click the Full Text Indexing tab. The Full-Text Indexing tab is to set up an indexing schedule for creating full-text indexes and enabling fast searches and lookups in Exchange 2003. You can update existing indexes or completely rebuild an index. You can also take an existing index offline so that it cannot be searched by clients.

 Caution   Full indexing places a high demand on server processor utilization. Administrators should be sure to schedule indexing for off-peak usage time periods when the server is not in heavy use so that server performance is not impacted.

6. Click the Details tab. The Details tab gives the administrator a place to enter notes and keep a track record of notes about the mailbox store configuration. It also shows the creation date and the last time the mailbox store was modified.

7. Click the Policies tab. The Policies tab is used to check which policies apply to this mailbox store, but it does not allow modification of the policies.

8. Click OK to finish and create the new mailbox store. When prompted, click Yes to mount the new store and make it available for use.

Creating Public Folder Data Stores

Public folders are used by organizations to share information such as email messages and files among all Exchange users. This information is contained in the public folder store. A public folder store requires that a public folder tree, which is unique and assigned to a single public folder store, be associated with it. Each new Exchange server has one default public folder store named the Public Folder Store. The Public Folder Store supports the Exchange default public folder tree, which is named Public Folders in Exchange System Manager and All Public Folders in Outlook. Users can access this tree with MAPI-based clients, such as Outlook, and with HTTP-based clients, such as Microsoft Outlook Web Access. Only one Public Folder tree is in each Exchange organization and all the default public folder stores replicate this tree and its content among themselves.

 Note   Some organizations will need additional public folder stores. Administrators typically create additional public folder stores to share messages and files associated with certain roles, departments, or business units. Public folders also provide a way to share messages and files related to projects or business initiatives. Exchange performance is improved by placing public folder stores on different drives and servers. Administration is also simplified by allowing different sets of rules to be applied to different sets of users for items such as maintenance, security, storage limits, indexing, and policies.

In many ways, public folder stores are similar to mailbox stores. However, in contrast to mailbox stores, public folder stores can be replicated between servers. This allows users to access the public folder data on multiple servers, distributing the load. The replication process also provides another data source for data recovery in case of a server failure.

To create a public folder store in Exchange System Manager, use the following steps:

1. Select the Exchange server to manage. Right-click the necessary storage group, select New, and then click Public Store.

 Note To create a public folder store, a public tree must be available for use. If one isn't available, an information dialog box will appear, notifying the administrator that a public folder tree is needed before a public folder store can be created. If this is the case, see Lesson 7, "Using and Managing Public Folders" for instructions.

2. After the Properties dialog page appears (as shown in Figure 4.4), type a name for the public folder into the Name field on the General tab. Click Browse and then use the Select a Public Folder Tree dialog box to choose a public folder tree to associate with the public folder store.

3. Click the Database tab. If changes to the default database location are needed, change them here. The database maintenance schedule can also be changed on this page by clicking the Customize button and using the Schedule grid to set a new time.

4. Click the Replication tab to set replication intervals and limits for all folders in the public folder store. Replicas are useful for distributing user loads across servers, distributing public folders geographically across servers, or backing up public folder data.

5. Click the Limits tab to set database storage limits and configure data deletion settings, some of which are set on a per user basis. Some of the options available are Maximum Items Size, Warning Message Interval, and Age Limits for Retaining Folder Postings.

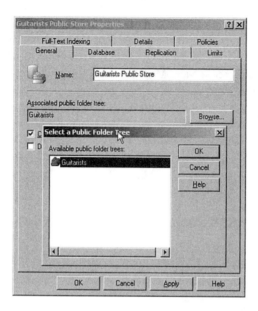

FIGURE 4.4   Associating a public folder tree with a public folder store.

6. Click OK to finish and create the new public folder store. When prompted, click Yes to mount the new store and make it available for use.

Caution   Administrators should notify users if an age limit is imposed on the public folder store. Otherwise, users could lose important messages and data when postings are automatically deleted.

Summary

Exchange System Manager (ESM) was first introduced with Exchange 2000 as a replacement for the Exchange Administrator used in previous versions of Exchange. Exchange System Manager 2003 is a specialized preconfigured Microsoft Management Console (MMC), Exchange System Manager.msc, which helps you manage your Exchange organization. With the capability to run along with other tools (Active Directory Users and Computers, Internet Services Manager, Event Viewer, and so on) in the same console using context menus (via the right mouse button), Exchange System Manager 2003 is an integrated toolbox for administrators who deal with all areas of Exchange server management, including policies, public folders, servers, and routing.

LESSON 5

Managing Mailboxes and Address Lists

This lesson delves into the procedures of basic mailbox and address list administration using step-by-step procedures for managing mailboxes, mailbox restrictions, address lists, and the address list and details templates.

Understanding Mailbox Administration

Mailbox administration is one of the main tasks of an Exchange administrator. The amount of time and effort spent managing the mailboxes can make or break an organization's efficiency and productivity. If the messaging system is not working, money, time, and effort are wasted as the organization tries to communicate within itself and with those outside the organization. As organizations depend on their messaging servers more and more, it is important that the Exchange server is available during peak office hours.

Mailboxes are created in Exchange as private storage areas for sending and receiving email messages and have configurable properties that control mailbox size limits, permissions, and mail delivery. Typically, when a user account is created in Active Directory, a mailbox is created for that user. If for some reason a mailbox was not created for an existing user, it can be done after the fact.

Managing Mailboxes

Mailbox administration is a straightforward process but takes a lot of an administrator's time during the day. Mailboxes can be created during the setup of a user account or can be added to existing user accounts as needed. If an existing user account needs a mailbox, you can create a mailbox using the following steps:

1. In Active Directory Users and Computers, right-click a user's name and select Exchange Tasks to initiate the Exchange Task Wizard. Click Next at the Welcome page. (If you previously chose the option to not display the Welcome page, you will be directed to the Available Tasks screen.)

2. Under Available Tasks, select the Create Mailbox option and then click Next. The Create Mailbox Wizard dialog box will be displayed.

3. By default, the Exchange alias is set to the logon name. This option is changed by entering a new alias name.

4. If multiple Exchange servers are configured with an Information Store or if multiple mailbox stores have been configured, use the relevant drop-down list to specify the proper server or mailbox store that should be used.

5. Click Next and then click Finish to complete the mailbox addition to the user account.

Caution Remember, if multiple user accounts are selected for adding mailboxes, the Exchange alias will be set to the user's logon name and cannot be changed. The Exchange alias can be changed only if a single user account is having a mailbox added.

Removing Mailboxes from User Accounts

Removing mailboxes from user accounts is just as easy. When mailboxes are removed from a user account, any email addresses associated with the account are deleted and the mailbox itself is marked for deletion. The deletion occurs according to the retention period set on the user account or the mailbox store. (See the instructions for Setting Deleted Item Retention Time for mailboxes later in this lesson for details.) You can remove a user account mailbox by completing the following steps:

1. In Active Directory Users and Computers, select the user whose mailbox will be removed. With the username highlighted, right-click and then select Exchange Tasks to start the Exchange Task Wizard. If a Welcome page appears, click Next.

2. As shown in Figure 5.1, under the Available Tasks, select Delete Mailbox and then click Next.

3. Click Next and then Finish, marking the mailbox for deletion.

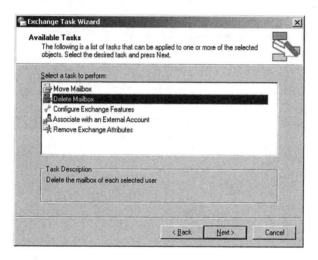

FIGURE 5.1   Deleting a mailbox using the Exchange Task Wizard.

Viewing Mailbox Size and Message Counts

Administrators may want to periodically check the size of mailboxes and the number of messages within a mailbox store. Using Exchange System

Manager (ESM), the mailbox sizes and message counts can be viewed in
a few quick steps:

1. In ESM, within the administrative or routing groups, select the
   Servers node that you want to manage by first expanding the
   Administrative Groups. Next, expand the First Administrative
   Group and then select and expand the Servers node.

2. Double-click the Exchange server to manage, and a list of available storage groups on the server will appear in the left pane of
   the console.

3. Expand the storage groups and mailbox stores until the Mailboxes node to manage appears in the left pane of the console. In
   the right console pane, a summary list of mailboxes contained in
   the mailbox store will be present, as shown in Figure 5.2.

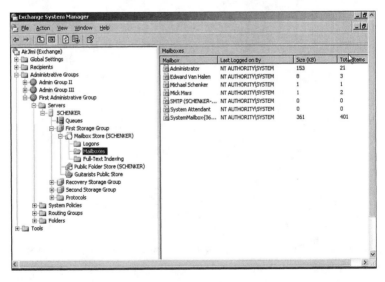

FIGURE 5.2   Viewing the mailboxes contained within a mailbox
store.

Setting Mailbox Restrictions

Mailbox properties are applied to set permissions, mail delivery restrictions, and storage limits. Although some settings are set globally at the server level during user creation, the configuration settings apply to the mailbox properties of individual mailboxes. Techniques for changing the configuration settings will be explored in this section. Let's start by looking at mailbox permissions and rights.

Mailbox rights let administrators configure access rights per mailbox. When administrators create new mailbox-enabled accounts in Active Directory, they do not have inherited mailbox rights. Only a special identity object, SELF, is granted full mailbox access and read rights. These access rights grant the users privileges to access their account and read, send, or delete mail messages. Administrators can manage mailboxes because they are members of the Administrators group, which is the owner of the mailboxes. As owners of the mailboxes, administrators can do tasks such as view mailbox information or delete mailboxes.

Viewing Mail Access Rights

To view the mail access rights and/or make changes, perform the following steps:

1. In Active Directory Users and Computers, double-click the mail-enabled user account to open the Properties page.

2. Click the Exchange Advanced tab and then click Mailbox Rights. This displays the Permissions For page shown in Figure 5.3.

Note Administrators may see only the SELF user shown in the Permissions For page. This will occur until the user logs on or receives mail. To resolve, log on to the mailbox using an OWA session (http://server-name/exchange/username). This creates the mailbox in the store, which calculates the inherited permissions and stamps them on the store's copy of the mailbox security descriptor. The Permission For page should now look similar to Figure 5.3.

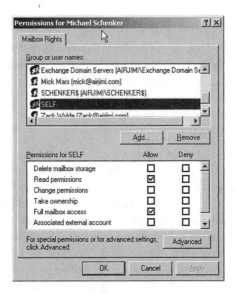

FIGURE 5.3   Configuring mailbox rights with the Permissions For dialog box.

3. Select the user or group whose rights you want to change and then use the Permissions lists to allow or deny rights. If the rights have been inherited, they will appear grayed out. To override inherited rights, select the opposite permissions.

4. Additional users or groups can be added by clicking the Add button. Select the computers, users, or groups to add and then configure the appropriate rights in the permissions area.

5. Click OK and then click OK again to finish.

Configuring Mail Retention Settings

When a user deletes an email in an Exchange server-based email organization, the email is not actually deleted in the information store. The message is marked as hidden and kept for a set period of time. The set period of time is known as the deleted item retention period. Default Retention settings are defined globally in default server settings or can be overridden on a per user basis. To configure the settings on an individual mailbox, use the following steps:

1. In Active Directory Users and Computers, double-click the mail-enabled user account to open the Properties page.

2. Click the Exchange General tab and then click the Storage Limits button to display the Storage Limits dialog box as shown in Figure 5.4.

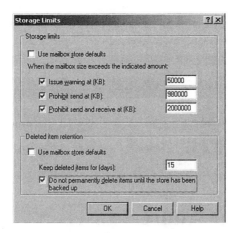

FIGURE 5.4 Specifying deleted item retention settings using the Storage Limits dialog box.

3. Uncheck the Use Mailbox Store Defaults box and enter the number of days to retain deleted items in the Keep Deleted Items For (Days) text field.

 Caution If the retention period is set to 0 days, messages are not retained and are immediately deleted. To make sure that deleted items are retained into an archive set, set the retention time to at least 14 days and be sure to check the option to not permanently delete messages before the mail store has been backed up, as shown in Figure 5.4.

4. Click OK to apply the changes.

Hiding a Mailbox from the Global Address List

Occasionally, administrators may want to hide a mailbox so that it will not appear in the Global Address List (GAL) or any other address list in an organization. For example, a company project may have a group of consultants from outside the organization working for you who need to be in communication with each other but not others within your organization, or you may have company internal mailboxes that are used only for certain purposes. Hiding the mailbox prevents the GAL from being cluttered with the special mailbox that most email users will not use. Hiding the mailbox is done with a few simple steps:

1. In Active Directory Users and Computers, double-click the mail-enabled user account to open the Properties page.

2. Click the Exchange Advanced tab and select Hide from Exchange Address Lists.

3. Click OK to complete hiding the mailbox.

Managing Address Lists

Exchange administrators use address lists to organize and manage email recipients. An address list is a folder that contains a dynamic listing of the Exchange 2003-enabled objects in an organization. Administrators are able to define address lists based on Active Directory attributes such as business unit, location, or other criteria. When administrators define a particular business unit, location, or department on a user account, the user is automatically made a member of that address list. This makes it easier for people to find the person or the distribution list to which they want to send an email message.

Exchange creates several default address lists during the setup process. In addition to the Global Address List (all mail-enabled users, groups, and contacts) and the Offline Address List (an offline address list of all mail-enabled users, groups, and contacts), Exchange creates the following lists:

- All Contacts—Lists all mail-enabled contacts.

- All Groups—Lists all mail-enabled groups.

- All Users—Lists all mail-enabled users.

- All Public Folders—Lists all public folders.

Typically, the offline address list and the global address list are the lists used most frequently in an organization.

 Tip When you create new address lists, use naming conventions that indicate the content of the list. Because most often people send messages to people in their own department, such as Engineering, administrators should create address lists that organize people by department or location and describe the types of recipients in the list. For example, an address list created for the Engineering department called Engineering Department Email would be more effective and easier to use than an address list named Pocket Protector Group.

Setting Up New Address Lists

Administrators can create address lists for organizing email recipients by location, department, or other organizational criteria. For example, an administrator wants to create an address book to find all users who work in the Air Jimi company headquarters in Oakland, California. To configure an address book that can be viewed by users in their Outlook 2003 mail clients, complete the following steps:

1. Open System Manager and select the Recipients node in the console tree (left pane).

2. Expand the Recipients object by clicking the plus sign; then right-click the All Address Lists node, point to New, and select Address List.

3. Type a name that describes the list that you are creating. For example, type `Oakland Email Addresses`.

4. Click Filter Rules to select list membership criteria. On the General tab, click the check boxes for the users, groups, public folders, or contacts that should be displayed in the list. Clear the check boxes for unwanted items.

5. Click the Advanced tab, click Field, and then click one of the following attributes that you want to use for your address book filter: User, Contact, Group, or Public Folder. The administrator wants all Oakland email addresses, so click User and then select City.

6. Under the Condition label, select a condition that fits the type of information to search on. Here the administrator will select Condition Is (Exactly) and then type Oakland into the Value field. This will set the criteria to find email addresses at the Air Jimi Headquarters in Oakland. Next, click Add to complete the process.

7. After you have finished adding conditions, click Find Now. As shown in Figure 5.5, double-check that the list contains the correct users in the list and then click OK, Finish.

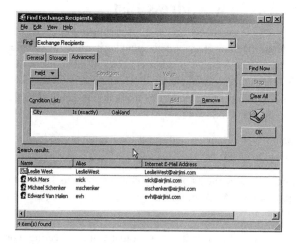

FIGURE 5.5 Specifying address list membership criteria and viewing search results using the Advanced tab.

The newly created address list is displayed in Exchange System Manager. To confirm that the address lists are configured properly and are available for users the next time they start Outlook, complete the following steps:

1. Log on to a workstation as a user and start Outlook.

2. Click New, click Mail Message, and then click To.

3. Click the down arrow in the Show Names From box and confirm that the new address book is displayed under All Address Lists.

Administrators will often want to edit address lists. The properties of the default address lists cannot be changed, but the properties of lists created by administrators can be. To modify the properties of a list, follow these steps:

1. Open Exchange System Manager and select the Recipients node in the console tree (left pane). Expand the Recipients node by clicking the plus sign and then clicking the plus sign next to the All Address Lists node.

2. Right-click and then select Properties of the address list to modify. Next, click Modify to create a new filter for the address list.

3. On the General tab, select the appropriate users, groups, or contacts to be displayed in the recipients list. Use the Advanced tab to set address list limiting criteria.

4. After all the filters have been set for the list, click OK and then click Finish, completing the process and making the list available for users the next time they start Outlook.

Working with Address Book Templates

Address book and Details templates specify how recipient information appears in the Address Book and can be customized by administrators to respond to requests of users or to meet organizational needs for streamlining information. The graphical interface is unique for each type of recipient and has a predefined set of controls that define the interface. The controls can be modified in width, height, location, and so on to change the way information is displayed in the Address Book view.

Modifying templates creates a custom view of the standard templates that are available to all users in Exchange. Changes to the template can be previewed as they are made, and if template changes are unsatisfactory, the original templates can always be restored. To change the look and feel of a template, use the following steps:

1. Open Exchange System Manager and select the Recipients node in the console tree (left pane). Expand the Recipients node by clicking the plus sign and then click the plus sign next to the Details node. Select the appropriate template language, and a list of available templates will be displayed in the right console pane.

2. Double-click the template to modify it. Select the Templates tab and wait while ESM parses the template values and any associated Active Directory information. A list of control sets and control values for the template will appear. Clicking Test will provide a preview of the template and give you a chance to review the template before making changes.

3. To add a new control to the template, click Add and then choose the appropriate control set. Set the correct properties for the control and click OK. Next, click Test to preview the modifications. To remove a control set, highlight the control set and click Remove.

4. Existing control sets can be update within the Templates tab by selecting the control set and clicking Modify. Make any changes and then click OK. Test the appearance of the dialog box configuration by clicking the Test button and inspecting the customized view. If unwanted modifications are accidentally saved, click Original and then click Yes to restore original settings.

5. Repeat steps 2, 3, and 4 to fine-tune the view. If required, use the Move Up and Move Down option to place the control sets in the scrolling list.

6. When you are satisfied with the modifications, click OK. Be sure to rebuild the address lists as described next in this lesson.

Note Don't forget to use the Administrative Note field on the Details tab to track and document template information. It is a useful troubleshooting tool when you are trying to figure out what changes were made to the template controls days, weeks, or months later and you don't remember!

Rebuilding the address list membership and configuration is another task administrators must do after making many changes to address lists and templates. The resynchronization process is fairly easy:

1. In Exchange System Manager, select and expand the Recipients node by clicking the plus sign; then select Recipient Update Services (RUS) to display the current RUS services in the right pane.

2. Select the appropriate domain or enterprise configuration by right-clicking and selecting Rebuild. When prompted, read the dialog warning information and then click Yes to begin the rebuilding process. Updates will be available for users the next time Outlook is opened for use.

Managing Offline Address Lists

Offline address lists are available only when Outlook users are working offline and not connected to the Exchange Server. Administrators configure offline address lists differently from online address books. First, they must configure the email client machine to use personal folders or to have a local copy of the server mailbox. Then the client system must be configured to use offline address lists. Use the following steps to configure Outlook 2003 on the client:

1. Open Outlook 2003 and select Tools, Send/Receive, and Download Address Book to display the Address Book dialog box. Next, select Download Changes Since Last Send/Receive to download only items that have changes since the last synchronization. Uncheck this option to perform a full address book download, which requires more download time.

2. Next, specify whether to download Full Details (all address details, but with a longer download time) or No Details (no address details, but selecting this option reduces download time). If multiple address books are available, pick which book to download in the Choose Address Book drop-down list.

3. Click OK to finish the process.

Creating New Offline Address Lists

The Default Offline Address List contains all the addresses listed in the global address list. For better organization and user productivity, administrators can create additional offline address books if necessary. To create a new offline address list, use the following steps:

1. In ESM, expand the Recipients node by clicking the plus sign; then right-click the Offline Address Lists node, point to New, and click Offline Address List.

2. Type a name for the offline address list; the name will be displayed in Active Directory and will be used to manage the offline address book in Exchange System Manager. Outlook does not use this name.

3. To select a server for the offline address book, click Browse. Type the name of the preferred server or use the Advanced option to search for a server. Click Next to continue.

4. Use Add and Remove to select address lists for Exchange Server 2003 to use as sources for the offline address book. When you are finished selecting items for the address list, click the Next Button twice and then click Finish to conclude the Offline Address List Wizard.

Rebuilding Offline Address Lists

Exchange Server 2003 configures the Active Directory object for the offline address book, and the offline address book files are created the next time the Exchange store maintenance processes run.

When new offline address books are created, the address lists must be rebuilt so that the updates are available to Outlook users. By default, Offline address books are automatically rebuilt daily at 5:00 a.m., yet they can be rebuilt manually if needed. To change the time when the rebuild occurs, perform the following steps:

1. In ESM, expand the Recipients node by clicking the plus sign; then select the Offline Address Lists node. Right-click the address list to modify and click Properties.

2. On the General tab, select one of the time intervals in the Update Interval drop-down list. To create a specific update interval setting, click Customize and then define a rebuild schedule.

3. If required, click the check boxes for Exchange 4.0 and 5.0 compatibility and then click OK. Otherwise, just click OK to finish modifying the rebuild schedule.

 Tip   Enabling offline address list support for Exchange 4.0 and 5.0 will affect the performance of Exchange 2003. If backward compatibility is not required, leave this option disabled to maximize Exchange 2003 performance.

A manual rebuild of an address list can be performed using the following steps:

1. In ESM, expand the Recipients node by clicking the plus sign; then select the Offline Address Lists node. Right-click the address list to manually rebuild and click Rebuild.

2. When prompted to confirm the rebuild, click Yes to start the rebuild process. Updates will be available the next time users open Outlook.

Summary

In this lesson, you learned the basic steps and task for creating, deleting, and managing mailboxes, setting mailbox restrictions, creating and modifying online and offline address lists, and manipulating the address list and details templates to create organization-specific, custom address book views. Because mailbox administration is one of the main tasks of an Exchange administrator, the amount of time and effort spent managing the mailboxes makes the difference between an average administrator and a superstar administrator.

LESSON 6
Managing Administrative Groups and Routing Groups

This lesson delves into the basic setup and configuration procedures of administrative groups, routing groups, and connectors in Exchange 2003.

Working with Administrative Groups

Administrators use Administrative Groups to organize and manage the Exchange architecture and resources and help describe the logical structure of the Exchange organization. Unlike Exchange 5.5, Exchange 2000 and 2003 split the concept of a site into logical and physical components. Administrative groups define a logical grouping of servers and other objects.

Administrative groups can contain any Exchange objects, such as servers, routing groups, public folder trees, and policies, and are useful for managing permissions. Small- and medium-sized organizations can use administrative groups, but large organizations with several company locations are better suited to make use of such groups. In large organizations, administrators can create an administrative group for each location or department and delegate specific permissions and define system policies for the administrative groups and the objects in the group.

Displaying Administrative Groups

To simplify the initial Exchange management process, administrative groups are not automatically displayed. Administrators must configure the Exchange organization to display administrative groups. When the Administrative Groups container is visible, additional administrative groups can be created. Administrative groups can be enabled using the following steps:

1. In ESM, right-click the Exchange organization (the root or parent node in the left pane) and then click Properties. On the General tab, select Display Administrative groups.

2. Restart ESM to apply the changes and enable administrative groups and containers for the current operating mode.

Management of Administrative Groups depends on whether Exchange 2003 is running in mixed mode, supporting pre-Exchange 2000 server installations, or running in native mode, supporting only Exchange 2000 Server and Exchange Server 2003. By default, Exchange 2003 is installed with the operation mode set to mixed mode to support interoperability with Exchange 5.0 and Exchange 5.5. This configuration limits the administrative group management capabilities of Exchange 2003 to those of Exchange 5.5 Server's management of sites, with each administrative group having only one functional routing group, even if additional routing groups are installed. Another limiting factor is the inability to move mailboxes from a server in one administrative group to a server in another administrative group. Moreover, additional limitations exist when Exchange 2003 is installed in an Exchange 5.5 site—such as limited ESM capability of the Exchange 5.5 Server, the inability to edit Exchange 5.5 objects directly through Active Directory, and the inability to use query-based distribution groups that require Windows 2003 domains and the native mode operation of Exchange with at least Exchange 2000 and SP3 or later.

Tip In Exchange 2003 Server Service Pack 1 (SP1), an updated feature allows administrators to move mailboxes between administrative groups in mixed mode. Rather than an administration tool that is used daily, this feature is best used during a site consolidation or server migration. For more information, download and read Microsoft's Exchange Server 2003 Deployment Guide at http://www.microsoft.com/downloads/details.aspx?FamilyID=77B6D819-+C7B3-42D1-8FBB-FE6339FFA1ED&displaylang=en.

Switching Operational Modes

A new Exchange 2003 organization runs in mixed mode until it is promoted to native mode. An Exchange organization can be promoted to native mode only if no servers are running Exchange 5.5 (or earlier) and the Site Replication Service (SRS) is not running. Administrators must upgrade all servers and any connectors before switching to native mode. Moreover, switching an organization to native mode is a one-way operation; the operational mode cannot be switched back to mixed mode and Exchange 2003 will not work with any Exchange 5.5 or 5.0 sites that are part of the organization. To switch the operational mode, use the following steps:

1. In Exchange System Manager, right-click your Exchange organization and then select Properties.

2. On the General tab of the Properties box, the Operation Mode field shows the current operational mode as Mixed Mode or Native Mode. Click Change Mode; confirm switching the operational mode by clicking Yes.

    Remember that this is a one-way change; you can't change back to mixed mode.

Adding Administrative Groups

Let's look at some of the administrative tasks, such as creating new groups, moving and copying between groups, and deleting and renaming administrative groups. Exchange 2003 creates a default administrative group called the First Administrative Group during the first installation of Exchange. Additional groups can be created by using the following steps:

1. In ESM, right-click Administrative Groups, point to New, and then select Administrative Group.

2. On the General tab, type in a name for the new group and then click OK.

Exchange creates the new group but doesn't assign any containers or servers to the new group. Servers, routing groups, system policies, and public folders can be added manually to an administrative group in System Manager by right-clicking the administrative group, pointing to New, and then selecting the new container type to add. Remember, only one of each container type can exist in an administrative group.

Moving and Copying Objects Between Groups

Moving and copying among administrative groups involves objects such as public folders and system policies; servers and containers cannot be moved. By default, objects can be moved only between containers of the same type. Moving a system policy from one system policy container to another system policy container in a different administrative group is allowed, but moving a system policy into a public folder container is prohibited. To copy objects between groups, follow these steps:

1. In ESM, expand the Administrative Groups by clicking the plus sign next to the node. Next, expand the administrative group and containers to work with.

2. Right-click the source object and select Copy.

3. Right-click the target container and select Paste.

Moving an object is just as easy:

1. In ESM, expand the Administrative Groups by clicking the plus sign next to the node. Next, expand the administrative group and containers to work with.

2. Right-click the source object and select Cut.

3. Right-click the target container and select Paste.

Renaming and Deleting Administrative Groups

Administrators may need to delete or rename administrative groups as part of their management task. Perform the following steps to rename an administrative group:

1. In ESM, expand Administrative Groups.

2. Right-click the appropriate group and select Rename on the menu. Then type in a new name for the group and press Enter.

Deleting administrative groups can be performed after the containers are empty. It is good practice to move items to a new administrative group and make sure the items are no longer needed before deleting the administrative group. To delete an administrative group, use these steps:

1. In ESM, expand Administrative Groups, right-click the administrative group that you want to delete, and then click Delete.

2. When prompted, click Yes to confirm the deletion.

Working with Routing Groups

Routing groups define the physical network topology of the Exchange servers. A routing group is a logical collection of servers used to control mail flow and public folder referrals. All servers in a routing group communicate and transfer messages directly to one another. For example, if a company has branch offices in Oakland and Detroit, each office may have its own routing group. To communicate between the two locations, the routing groups are connected with connectors such as the X.400 connector, the SMTP connector, and the Exchange Routing Group connector. In a routing group, servers communicate and transfer messages as outlined in the following steps::

1. A user in your Exchange organization sends mail to another user.

2. Via SMTP, the mail is submitted to the SMTP virtual server on the Exchange server on which the user's mailbox resides.

3. The Exchange server determines which server the recipient's mailbox resides on.

4. If the recipient's mailbox is on the same Exchange server, Exchange delivers the message to the recipient's mailbox. Otherwise, the first Exchange server sends the message to the recipient's home mailbox server, which then delivers the message to the recipient's mailbox.

Although all servers communicate with each other directly in a routing group, to facilitate communication between a server in one routing group and a server in another routing group, an administrator must create a routing group connector. Although other connectors such as SMTP or X.400 can be used for the connecting servers, the routing group connector is the preferred method of connecting routing groups because it was designed specifically for routing group connections:.

 Note In native mode, all servers in an Exchange organization are placed in a single routing group called the First Routing Group. Because the servers are in one routing group, the servers communicate directly with one another. In mixed mode, each Exchange 5.5 or earlier site becomes a routing group.

Enabling and Creating Routing Groups

Administrators must configure the Exchange organization to display routing groups. After configuring this setting, the routing groups container is visible, and additional routing groups can be created for the organization. Routing groups can be enabled using the following steps:

1. In ESM, right-click the Exchange organization and then click Properties. On the General tab, select Display Routing groups.

2. Restart Exchange System Manager to apply the changes and enable routing groups and containers for the current operating mode.

When a routing group is created, two containers, connectors and members, are displayed beneath the routing group. The connectors' container displays all connectors installed on the servers in the routing group. The members' container displays the servers in the routing group. By default, the first server installed in a routing group is the routing group master server.

Configuring routing groups is a multiple-step process: create the routing group, add member servers to the routing group, and then connect the routing group with a messaging connector. To create a routing group, complete the following steps:

1. In ESM, expand the Administrative Groups and select the administrative group to add the routing group to.

2. Right-click the Routing Groups node, point to New, and then select Routing Group.

3. On the General tab, type a descriptive name for the group and then click OK. Exchange creates the new routing group, but administrators will need to assign the servers and connectors.

Moving Servers Between Routing Groups

Administrators may want to move servers between routing groups to place those servers with the most reliable connections within the same routing group. Moving servers between routing groups is useful whenever a network topology changes, a site consolidation occurs, or servers are being centralized. In native mode, servers can move between routing groups that exist in different administrative groups. In mixed mode, however, administrators can move servers only between routing groups in the same administrative group. Moving servers is performed using the following steps:

1. In ESM, expand the routing group that currently has the server to be moved, and then expand the Members folder in that routing group.

2. Expand the target routing group that will be the new location for the server, and then expand the Members folder in that routing group.

3. In the Members folder of the source routing group, select the server and drag it to the Members folder of the target routing group for the server.

Renaming and Deleting Routing Groups

Administrators may also need to rename or delete routing groups. Use the following steps to rename a routing group:

1. In ESM, expand the Administrative Groups and select the administrative group containing the routing group to work with.

2. Expand the Routing Groups container and then right-click the routing group to change and click Rename.

3. Type in a new name for the routing group and press Enter.

Deleting routing groups can be performed after the containers are empty. It is good practice to move member servers to a new routing group. To delete a routing group, use these steps:

1. In ESM, expand the Administrative Groups and select the administrative group containing the routing group to work with. Expand the Routing Groups container and then right-click the routing group to remove and click Delete.

2. When prompted, click Yes to confirm the deletion.

Configuring the X.400 Message Transfer Agent (MTA) and Parameters

X.400 is the only connector included with the setup of Exchange 2003. Improper configuration of the X.400 MTA can affect the performance of Exchange Server 2003. Although the MTA isn't responsible for message delivery, the MTA handles message transfers to servers within organizations and the Internet and sets the default values used by X.400 connectors in an organization. Typically, MTA credentials, the local server name and password, do not need to be changed. Should an administrator need to change the server identity, use the following steps to modify the credentials:

1. In ESM, expand the Administrators Group containing the server to modify. Expand the Servers node, expand the server to work with, and then expand Protocols.

2. Right-click X.400 and then select Properties to display the Properties page, as shown in Figure 6.1.

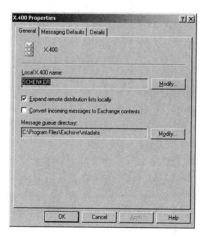

FIGURE 6.1   Using the X.400 Properties dialog box to set X.400 options.

3. Click Modify, type in a new name and password, and then click OK twice.

The dialog box contains check box options for expanding remote distribution lists locally and for converting incoming messages to Exchange contents. The optimal setting for expanding remote distribution lists locally is enabled by default. This option is rarely ever changed. The option to convert incoming messages to Exchange contents converts incoming messages to a MAPI-compatible format and should be used to troubleshoot receiving messages from outside messaging systems. By default, this option is unchecked and is disabled.

The Messaging Default tab of the X.400 properties is for configuring the default X.400 transport stack attributes. It contains configurable settings for options such as connection retry values (how server connects to other servers), reliable transfer service (RTS) values (how message data is transferred), association parameters (how established connections are handled), and transfer timeout values (how Non-Deliverable Receipts are generated).

The connection retry values are edited on the main Messaging Default tab. To access and edit the RTS and transfer timeout values, click the Additional Values button. Most of the defaults here are optimized for typical Exchange environments; if server performance is worse after making changes, restore default settings using the Reset Default Values buttons.

Configuring X.400 Connectors

Although more complex to use than other connectors, X.400 connectors are used to connect two routing groups because they incur less overhead than other connectors and use bandwidth more efficiently than other connectors when sending large messages. They are also useful for talking to a foreign X.400 messaging server; they can talk to TCP/IP X.400 protocol and the X.25 X.400 protocol. The TCP/IP X.400 connector works with standard TCP/IP protocols and is the most commonly used connector, so we'll look at configuring that option in this section.

Creating a TCP/IP X.400 Stack

Before installing the X.400 connector, a X.400 stack must be installed and configured. Create a TCP/IP X.400 stack by performing the following steps:

1. In ESM, expand the administrative group to work with. Expand the Servers node and then expand the server to work with.

2. Expand Protocols and then right-click X.400. Point to New and then select TCP/IP X.400 Service Transport Stack. On the General tab, type a descriptive name for the stack. The default naming convention is TCP (servername). Be sure to change the name now; it can't be changed later.

3. If applications other than Exchange will be using the stack, configure the OSI settings and then click OK. Otherwise, click OK to complete the stack creation.

Creating an X.400 Connector

After the stack has been created, one or more X.400 connectors can be created to transport messages to remote email hosts. The connector creates a direct link between a server in one routing group and a server in another routing group or organization. After the necessary stacks have been created on both sides of the connection, perform the following steps:

1. In ESM, expand the administrative group to work with. If available, expand the Routing Groups node and then expand the routing group to use as the connection creator.

2. Right-click Connectors, select New, and then choose TCP X.400 Connector. On the General tab, type a descriptive name for the connector, as shown in Figure 6.2.

3. On the General tab, under Remote X.400 name, click Modify to open the Remote Connection Credentials dialog box. In the Remote X.400 name field, type the name of the remote X.400 connector on the remote server. Typically, the remote connector

name defaults to the remote server name. Type the password for the remote X.400 connector into the password field and again in the Confirm Password field. Click OK.

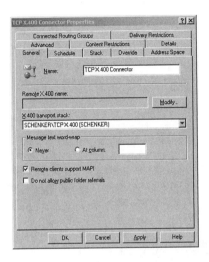

FIGURE 6.2   Using the Properties dialog box to configure the TCP X.400 connector.

4. On the General tab, select the appropriate X.400 Transport stack from the drop-down list.

5. Select the Address Space tab in the Properties dialog box. If two Exchange organizations are being connected, set the Connector scope as Entire Organization, click Add, and then set the address space properties and cost values. Lower-cost values mean higher priority for routing. If two routing groups are being connected, set the Connector scope as Routing Group, click Add, and then set the properties and set connector cost values (lower cost has the highest priority).

6. On the Connected Routing Groups tab, click Add. Then select the routing group to which you want to connect.

7. If the remote system is not an Exchange server, click the Advanced tab and clear the Allow Exchange contents check box. If the check box is not cleared, addresses on messages are in domain name form, not in X.400 form, and replies are not possible.

8. On the Stack tab for a TCP X.400 connector, select the Remote hostname and type the fully qualified domain name (FQDN) into the Address box, or select IP Address and type the remote server's IP address into the Address box.

9. Click the Schedule tab and select an appropriate time for the connector to run: Never (disable the connector), Always (continuous transfer over the connector), Selected Times (a custom schedule to run the connector), or Remote Initiated (transfer only when the remote server initiates the transfer).

10. If nondefault X.400 settings are required, click the Override tab and set custom values. Otherwise, click OK to install the connector.

After the routing group connector is installed, administrators may want to change additional settings such as delivery restrictions and advanced controls.

Configuring Routing Group Connectors

Routing group connectors are one-way routes for outgoing messages; messages travel outbound to the connected routing group. A routing group connector must exist in each routing group for the routing groups to communicate to each other and to send messages outbound to the other routing group. Although administrators can connect routing groups with an X.400 connector or SMTP connector, a routing group connector is the preferred connection method because this connector is designed and optimized for connection performance. Bridgehead servers, discussed later in this lesson, are the endpoints in the communication link between routing groups. To configure the options for a routing group connector, use the following steps:

1. In ESM, expand the routing group to use as the originator of the connection, right-click Connectors, select New, and then click Routing Group Connector.

2. On the General tab, type a descriptive name, such as OaklandToDetroit, for the routing group connector.

3. Using the Connects This Routing Group With drop-down list, select the destination routing groups to connect to.

4. In the Cost value field, assign an appropriate cost for the connector; the default value is 1.

5. If all servers in the local routing group will function as bridgehead servers, select Any Local Server Can Send Mail Over This Connector. Otherwise, select These Servers Can Send Mail Over This Connector and then click Add to specify servers in the local routing group that can function as bridgehead servers for this connector.

6. On the Remote Bridgehead tab, click Add, and then select the remote bridgehead server from the list of servers in the routing group to which you are connecting. Click OK to create the connector.

 Tip If a message is displayed asking to create a routing group connector in the remote routing group, click Yes. This new routing group connector permits the remote routing group to send messages to the local routing group.

After the routing group connector is installed, administrators may want to change additional settings, such as delivery options, delivery restrictions, and content restrictions.

Configuring SMTP Connectors

SMTP connectors are another type of connector available in Exchange 2003 and are used to transfer messages between local bridgehead servers and remote servers. SMTP connectors are more complex to use than routing group connectors, yet they have distinct advantages: stronger authentication and encryption, smart host support, DNS mail exchanger record support, and Extended SMTP support. Multiple SMTP connectors can also be configured for load balancing and providing highly available email architecture. Because an SMTP connector creates an isolated route for mail delivery, it eases administration and troubleshooting of mail flow problems. To configure an SMTP connector, perform the following steps:

1. In ESM, expand the routing group to work with, right-click Connectors, select New, and then click SMTP Connector. The Properties dialog box for the new connector appears.

2. On the General tab, type a descriptive name for the connector.

3. To use the DNS settings configured on the SMTP virtual server that is hosting the connector, select Use DNS to Route to Each Address Space on This Connector. (DNS resolves the IP address of the remote SMTP server.)

4. To use a smart host routing, select Forward All Mail Through This Connector to the Following Smart Hosts. (Smart host handles DNS resolution and mail delivery.)

5. On the General tab, click Add and then add a bridgehead server and an SMTP virtual server as shown in Figure 6.3. Repeat to use additional bridgehead servers.

6. Click the Address Space tab. If two Exchange organizations are being connected, set the Connector scope as Entire Organization and then click Add to configure an SMTP address space with the appropriate Cost. If two routing groups are being connected, set the Connector Scope to Routing Groups and then click Add to configure an SMTP address space and a Cost. After this is done, click the Routing Group tab and select the routing group to connect.

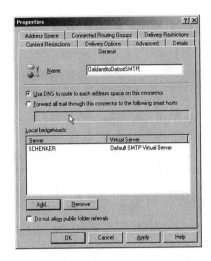

Figure 6.3 Using the Properties dialog box to configure SMTP connector settings.

7. If message relaying to other routing groups or organization is not needed, click OK to install the connector. Otherwise, click the Allow Messages to be Relayed to These Domains check box and then click OK to install the connector.

After the SMTP connector is installed, administrators may want to change additional settings, such as delivery options, outbound security, delivery and content restrictions, and other advanced controls.

Managing Connectors

Bridgehead servers act as the communication relays for routing groups. They are defined both remotely—the destination of email messages—and locally—the source of email messages. Each connector handles bridgehead connectors differently. Routing group connectors can have several local bridgeheads and one remote bridgehead and can be created using the steps described in the section "Configuring Routing Group Connectors" in this lesson. SMTP connectors can have more than one local bridgehead and use smart hosts or DNS MX records to locate remote mail servers. To set up, use the procedures in the section "Configuring SMTP Connectors" in this lesson. X.400 connectors have a one-to-one setup: one local and one remote bridgehead server. This configuration is limiting, and multiple connectors must be load balancing and fault tolerant. X.400 bridgehead servers are configured through the local and remote X.400 names designated for the connector.

For all connectors, administrative tasks, such as content restrictions, delivery restrictions, and removing and disabling connectors, are performed using very similar administrative steps.

Enabling Content Restrictions

Content restrictions set priority, allowed types, and sizes for transferred messages by a connector. To enable content restrictions, use the following steps:

1. In ESM, navigate to the Connectors container, right-click the appropriate connector, and select Properties. Then click the Content Restrictions tab.

2. Click the check boxes to set options for message priorities, message types, and maximum message size. Click OK when you're finished setting the options.

Enabling Delivery Restrictions

Delivery restrictions are used to accept or reject messages based on the sender's email address before being transferred over the connector. No restrictions are set, by default, allowing all messages to be delivered. To configure connectors to reject messages from specific senders, follow these steps:

1. In ESM, navigate to the Connectors container. Expand the Connectors container, right-click the connector that you want to work with, and then click Properties.

2. Click the Delivery Restrictions tab. Under Reject messages from, click Add.

3. In the Select Recipient dialog box, click the users, contacts, and groups whose messages are to be rejected. All other senders are accepted automatically.

4. Click OK twice.

 Tip Selecting individual recipients can take extra time. To save time, press and hold down the Ctrl key as you select a group of recipients.

Disabling Connectors

Connectors can be disabled or removed at any time. To disable a connector, follow these steps:

1. In ESM, right-click the connector to disable and then click Properties.

2. To disable an SMTP connector or a routing group connector, click the Delivery Options tab. Under the Specify When Messages Are Sent Through This Connector option, in Connection Time, select Never Run from the drop-down list. To disable a X.400 connector, click the Schedule tab and then click Never.

3. Click OK to complete disabling the connector.

 Removing Connectors   Although not recommended, connectors can also be removed. To remove a connector, use these steps:

   1. In ESM, navigate to the Connectors container, right-click the connector to remove, and then click Delete.

   2. When prompted to delete the connector, click Yes.

Summary

Administrative Groups, Routing Groups, and Routing Group Connectors are responsible for message delivery internally and externally. They control the way messages flow between servers in the organization and to other servers outside the organization. The organizational routing topology, built on defined routing groups and connectors, determines the path that messages take to reach their final destination. With proper configuration, your messaging environment will run like a well-oiled machine.

LESSON 7
Using and Managing Public Folders

This lesson delves into the basic setup, administrative tasks, and usage of public folders in Exchange 2003.

Using and Accessing Public Folders

Public folders are often underutilized by companies and organizations. Many administrators won't take the time to understand, configure, and deploy public folders. This is a big mistake because public folders enhance an organization's ability to disseminate company information, company vision and initiatives, and the capability to collaborate on projects.

Public folders are used to share files and email messages within an organization and can have different names, such as Marketing, Engineering, and CompanyInfo, each with special access restrictions. For example, the Finance public folder is available only to Finance personnel and the Project Management public folder is available only to project management folks, but the CompanyInfo public folder is accessible to all company employees.

Public folders are stored in an organizational structure called a public folder tree. By design, administrators must create a public folder tree before creating a public folder store, and users can access public folder trees only when folders are part of a public folder store. The default public folder tree is accessible only through MAPI clients, such as Outlook 2003, whereas other public folder trees can be accessed with web browsers, Microsoft applications, or the Exchange System Manager (ESM).

Exchange 2003 makes it easy to access public folders for users both in the office and on the road. Public folders can be accessed via email clients, the Exchange information store, and the Internet.

Although users can access public folders with any MAPI-compliant email client, the recommended email client is Outlook 2003. If the email client is configured for Exchange 2003 Server, users of Outlook 2003 will have access to the public folders tree but not to alternative public folder trees. If Outlook 2003 is configured for Internet usage, IMAP must be configured to access public folders. If Outlook is configured properly, users can access public folders in Outlook 2003 using the following steps:

1. Open Outlook 2003. If the folder list is not displayed, click Go and then select Folder List.

2. In the Folder List, expand the public folders and then expand All Public Folders to display all available top-level public folders.

Verifying HTTP Virtual Server Settings

Users can also access public folders via the company intranet or the World Wide Web and can create and/or manage folders and their contents. Using an HTTP virtual server in Exchange 2003 and a web browser, users can access public folders by typing a URL, http://{servername}/public, where servername is the name of the virtual server and public is the default name of the Public Folder web share. With this access method, alternative public folders can also be accessed. Although Exchange 2003 automatically configures web shares and access controls, it is always a good idea to double-check the settings. Use the following steps to check the configuration:

1. In ESM, expand the Server node to work with and then expand the Protocols node. Expand the HTTP node and then expand Exchange Virtual server to display a list of Web shares.

2. Right-click Public and then select Properties. In the Public Properties dialog box, select the Access tab to check application and access permissions. Exchange sets default folder access per-

missions for read, write, directory browsing, and script source access. To prevent application access, Execute Permissions should be set to None.

3. Click OK to finish configuring access properties.

 Tip Most problems accessing public folders via the web are caused by incorrect settings. Most changes are accidental. Restore settings to the default when you're troubleshooting; most likely, users will then have access again.

Accessing Public Folders Through the Exchange Information Store

Public folders can also be accessed through the Exchange Information Store using the network path \\.\BackOfficeStorage. This path has a mailbox folder that is the root for all mailboxes on the server, a domain folder for all available domains, and a Public Folders folder that is the root of the default public folder tree. Using the directory command DIR, administrators can display the contents of the Information Store. For example, in the Pandora Networks domain, administrators would type **dir** "\\.\\BackOfficeStorage\PandoraNetworks.com\Public Folders". Be sure to include the quotes or an error may be generated because of the space in the public folder name.

Managing Public Folders

A public folder tree must be created and added to a public folder store before authorized users can create subfolders within a tree. The default tree is automatically created and managed by Exchange 2003; it cannot be created, deleted, or modified (only other public folder trees can be created, modified, or deleted) and is stored in the default container in the Exchange organization. Additional containers must be created in Exchange, if a container other than the default is desired. Administrators need to create additional containers only if administrative groups are being utilized, and administrators have the option of adding a public folders container to every administrative group created after the first administrative group.

Creating Public Folder Containers and Trees

Containers are created using the following steps:

1. In ESM, expand the administrative groups and then expand the administrative group to work with.

2. If a Folders node is displayed, a public folder tree already exists. If a Public Folders node is not displayed, right-click the administrative group, select New, and then select Public Folders Container.

3. You can now create public folder trees in the container.

Create a new public folder tree using the following steps:

1. In ESM, expand administrative groups and select the group to work with. In the left pane, right-click Folders, select New, and then select Public Folder Tree.

2. Type a descriptive name, without spaces, for the public folder tree (this makes it easier to access via web browsers) and then Click OK. Be sure to associate the new tree with a public folder store as discussed in the section "Creating Public Folder Data Stores" of Lesson 4.

3. Exit ESM and re-open to view the new public folder.

Creating Public Folders with Exchange System Manager

After the public folder tree is created and associated with a public folder store, new subfolders can be created by authorized users in Exchange System Manager, Internet Explorer, or Outlook 2003. Administrators can create public folders in Exchange System Manager using the following steps:

1. In ESM, expand administrative groups and select the group to work with. Next, expand the folders and then right-click the public folder tree to work with and select New, Public Folder. A properties dialog box will be displayed, as shown in Figure 7.1.

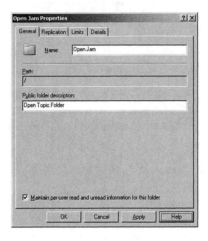

FIGURE 7.1   Creating public folders in Exchange System Manager.

2. Type a descriptive name for the new public folder into the Name field and then add a description in the Public Folder Description field. The name used for the public folder is also used for the email address of the public folder and is used to send messages to the folder.

3. On the Replication tab, check the default option settings. By default, the folder is replicated to the default public store for the public tree. To replicate the folder to another server in the organization, click Add, select an additional public store to use, and then click OK. Repeat this step as necessary to include other servers.

4. Determine how items are prioritized for replication by selecting a delivery priority:

   • Not Urgent—Messages with this low importance priority are replicated after messages with higher priority.

- Normal—This is the default replication setting. Messages with this priority are replicated before Not Urgent priority messages.

- Urgent—Messages with this priority are replicated before any other messages. Overuse of this priority can cause performance problems and folder update delays in Exchange, so use this setting wisely.

5. On the Limits tab, set individual message limits or select Use Public Store Defaults.

6. Click OK to complete the configuration.

After the basic setup is complete, folder creators may want to configure additional options for replication settings, message limits, client permissions and active directory rights, or designate public folder administrators.

Creating Public Folders in Outlook

Creating folders in Outlook 2003 is just as easy for both authorized users and administrators. Create folders using these steps:

1. Open Outlook 2003. Display the Folder List view and then expand the Public Folders in the Folder List. Right-click the top-level folder where you want to create the public folder.

2. Select New Folder. Type a descriptive name for the public folder and select the type of items to be placed in the folder via the Folder Contains drop-down list. Click OK to complete the folder creation.

After the folder creation is complete, folder creators may want to configure additional options for replication settings, message limits, client permissions and active directory rights, or designate public folder administrators.

Creating Public Folders Using Internet Explorer

Authorized users and administrators can also set up public folders using Microsoft Internet Explorer 5.0 and later (as long as the public folder tree is configured for web sharing.) To set up Public Folders using Internet Explorer, follow these steps:

1. Type the URL of the public folder tree into the address field of Internet Explorer. It will look similar to this: **http://{servername}/public**. Log in, if prompted to do so.

2. In the browser window, right-click the top-level folder where you want to create a public folder and select New Folder.

3. Type a descriptive name for the public folder and select the type of items to be placed in the folder via the Folder Contains drop-down list. Click OK to complete the folder creation.

After the folder creation is complete, folder creators may want to configure additional options for replication settings, message limits, client permissions and active directory rights, or designate public folder administrators.

Adding Items to Public Folders Using Exchange System Manager

After the folders are created and configured, items can be posted to them using Exchange System Manager, Internet Explorer, or Outlook.

Use the following steps to post items in Exchange System Manager:

1. Open ESM, select and expand Administrative Groups and then the administrative group to work with. Expand Folders, expand the Public Folder tree to work with, and then select the folder to post to.

2. Select the Content tab. A Post dialog box will appear. Click New to open OWA and display a Post dialog box. If prompted to log in, do so.

3. Type in a subject for the message posting and then type in the message text. Attachments can be added if necessary. Click Post to submit the message to the public folder.

Adding Items to Public Folders Using Internet Explorer and Outlook

Authorized users can post items to public folders using Internet Explorer (5.0 or later) and Outlook. Use the following steps to add a message:

1. Enter the URL of the public folder tree into the address field of Internet Explorer, such as `http://{servername}/public`. Log in if prompted to do so. Click OK.

2. Select the folder to work in and click New.

3. Type in a subject for the message posting and then type in the message text. Attachments can be added if necessary. Click Post to submit the message to the public folder.

Using Outlook to post a message is just as easy; use the following steps:

1. In Outlook, click Go and then select Folder List. Expand Public Folders and then All Public Folders. Select the public folder to post a message in.

2. Click New, type in a subject for the message, and then type in the message text. Attachments can be added if necessary. Click Post to submit the message to the public folder.

Manipulating Public Folders

Because administrators manage Exchange, they have the task of managing and manipulating public folders as well. Using standard administrative procedures outlined in this section, public folders can be deleted, renamed, moved, copied, or recovered.

Deleting Public Folders in Exchange System Manager

Deleting a public folder removes the contents of the public folder and the contents of any subfolders. Be sure the data is not needed or archived before deleting a public folder. To delete a public folder, use these steps:

1. In ESM, right-click the folder to remove and then select Delete.

2. Click Yes to confirm the public folder removal.

Renaming Public Folders

An organization may want to change the naming convention of the public folders or rename a single public folder. Renaming a public folder is simple using the following steps:

1. In ESM, right-click the folder to rename and then select Rename.

2. Type in a new name and then press Enter.

Copying and moving a public folder can be performed only within the same public folder tree; copying or moving a public folder to a different tree is not supported.

Moving and Copying Public Folders

To move a public folder, follow these steps:

1. In ESM, right-click the public folder to relocate and select Cut.

2. Right-click the folder to move the public folder into and select Paste.

To copy a public folder, follow these steps:

1. In ESM, right-click the public folder to relocate and select Copy.

2. Right-click the folder to copy the public folder into and select Paste.

Recovering Deleted Public Folders

Public folders may be accidentally deleted and need to be recovered by administrators. This is possible as long as two conditions are met: a deleted items retention period has been set for the public folder store; and the deleted items retention period for the data store has not expired. If the two conditions are met, deleted folders can be recovered using the following steps:

1. Log in to the domain with administrator privileges. Open Outlook and access the Public Folders node, and then select the All Public Folders node or the node that contained the public folders.

2. In the Tools menu, select Recover Deleted Items. This action will pop up a Recover Deleted Items dialog box.

3. Select the folders to recover and then click Recover Selected Items.

4. Each top-level folder restored by the recovery process will have "Recovered" added to the end of the name of the folder. The recovery process adds Recovered to all the email addresses you have assigned to the folder.

Tip After the folder contents have been verified, administrators should restore the folder's original name via the rename process and also restore the original email address via the Email Addresses tab in the folder's Properties dialog box. This makes the public folder appear and operate just as it did before being deleted; public folder users will appreciate the extra effort.

Delegating Administrative Permissions

Although the Public Folder Store properties sheet allows administrators to create a broad set of permissions that applies to all public folders, administrators can also modify permissions on individual folders. Administrators can control whether users are allowed to edit and delete any items in the folder, only items that they have posted, or no items at all. Administrators can also grant users the right to post content to one folder, but not to another. By default, all users have permission to access a folder and read the contents. Users who log on to the network or use OWA have additional privileges that allow them to create subfolders, read, create, edit, and delete items in a folder.

To help administrators configure permissions, Microsoft has provided several predefined roles that administrators can select, rather than applying individual permissions. For example, assigning users the Reviewer role would allow them to read items only. The complete list of roles and their associated permissions are as follows:

- Owner—All permissions are granted. Users can create, read, modify, and delete permissions and create subfolders. Owners can change folder permissions as well.

- Publishing Editor—Grants create, read, modify, and delete permissions. Also allows creation of subfolders.

- Editor—Grants create, read, modify, and delete permissions.

- Publishing Author—Grants permission to create and read items and to edit or delete user-created items. Subfolders can also be created.

- Non-editing Author—Grants permission to create and read folder items.

- Reviewer—Grants read-only permission.

- Contributor—Grants permission to create items but not view folder contents.

- None—No permissions are granted in the folder.

Modifying Public Folder Client Permissions

Permissions over the folder are set through the properties sheet's Permissions tab. This tab contains two buttons: Client Permissions and Administrative Rights. To modify existing permissions or set new roles for users in an individual public folder, use the following steps:

1. In ESM, expand administrative groups and then expand the group to work with.

2. Expand the Folders node and then expand the public folder tree that contains the folder to work with. Right-click the public folder and then select Properties.

3. On the Permissions tab, click Client Permissions. The Client Permissions dialog box will appear, showing account names, roles, and permissions.

4. Click Add and select the name of the user who needs access. Then click Add to include the username in the Add Users List. Repeat as necessary. Click OK when you're finished.

5. In the Name and Role list, select one or more users whose permissions need modifying. Then assign the appropriate role or individual permissions.

6. Click OK when you're finished assigning permissions.

Modifying Public Folder Administrative Rights

The Administrative Rights button is used to configure and control who is an administrator over the folder. Administrators can set a few different advanced permissions for controlling access to the folder or modifying the folder itself. Typically, these settings are left unchanged. To set a folder's administrative rights, use the following steps:

1. In ESM, expand administrative groups and then expand the group to work with.

2. Expand the Folders node and then expand the public folder tree that contains the folder to work with. Right-click the public folder and then select Properties.

3. On the Permissions tab, click Administrative Rights. The Permissions dialog box will appear.

4. Via the Permissions dialog box, grant or deny administrative privileges as appropriate.

5. Click OK when you're finished assigning administrative rights.

Managing Public Folder Replication

The Public Folder Replication Agent (PFRA), part of the public information store service, manages public folder replication. Exchange 2003 activates background PFRA threads when starting the public folder store. The PFRA performs several tasks: maintaining folder replica lists, monitoring replication schedules, dispatching replication messages at scheduled times, sending status messages to servers ensuring receipt of all replicated data, generating backfill requests if a server misses a piece of data, and responding to other servers' backfill requests.

Configuring Public Folder Replication Settings

Every folder in a public folder tree has it own replication settings. Initially, the contents of a public folder are replicated only to the default public store for the tree. Although this is okay as a basic setup, administrators will want to replicate folders to additional public stores for easier user access and to optimize system performance. Use the following steps to configure public folder replication:

1. In ESM, expand administrative groups and then expand the group to work with.

2. Expand the Folder node and then expand the folder tree that contains the folder to replicate.

3. Right-click the folder and select Properties. Select the Replication tab and review where replicas are currently being created, as shown in Figure 7.2.

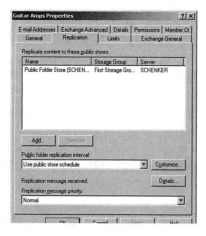

FIGURE 7.2   Configuring public folder replication settings in Exchange System Manager.

4. Replicate the folder to another server by clicking Add; then select another public folder store to use. Click OK to complete. Add additional replicas by repeating this step. Remember, you can have only one public folder store per server, so be sure to pick a public folder store that resides in a different storage group on another server.

5. The replication interval determines when folder changes are replicated. The schedule can be set to use the public store replication schedule or can be customized by selecting Use Custom Schedule and then clicking Customize. In the Schedule dialog box, select the preferred replication time.

6. The replication priority settings determine how items in the folder are replicated. Items in folders assigned a higher priority are replicated before messages in other folders. The three available priorities are Urgent, Not Urgent, and Normal, which is the default setting. Select the priority setting as appropriate for your organization. If you're unsure, accept the default settings.

7. Click OK to complete the configuration.

Removing Public Folder Replicas

Administrators may also want to remove a replica of a folder. To remove a replica, follow these steps:

1. In ESM, right-click the folder to work with and then select Properties.

2. Click the Replication tab to display the current replicas. To stop replication, select the store and click Remove.

Viewing Replication Status

The best way to check public folder replication is by checking the replication status. Administrators can look at individual public folders in Exchange 2003 and review the status of the folder replication details, such as server name, replication status, average replication time, and the last time a replication was received. Use the following steps to check the status for an individual public folder:

1. In ESM, right-click the folder to work with and then click the Replication tab.

2. Review the replication status in the Details pane on the right.

Summary

Although public folders are a very useful feature of Exchange and make Exchange more than just an email server, public folders are often under-utilized by companies and organizations. With a little effort, care, and maintenance, administrators can deploy public folders as the basis for information-sharing applications, such as document management and distribution, and to disseminate company information, company vision and initiatives, and to collaborate on projects across the entire organization regardless of location.

LESSON 8

Configuring and Managing Virtual Servers

This lesson delves into the configuration and management tasks of virtual servers in Exchange 2003.

Working with Virtual Servers

Exchange 2003 supports the Post Office Protocol 3 (POP3), Internet Message Access Protocol 4 (IMAP 4), Simple Mail Transfer Protocol (SMTP), and the Hypertext Transfer Protocol (HTTP). Some clients support all these protocols; others do not. To accommodate these differences in protocol usage, Exchange supports all these protocols. These protocols help establish how mail is transported within the organization and also from outside the Exchange organization. SMTP is the native protocol for mail delivery; Outlook users and Exchange servers use SMTP to deliver messages and data. The IMAP4 protocol is used to access mail and public and private folders; users log in to Exchange to download message headers and then read messages online. POP3 is a protocol for retrieving mail from remote servers; users log in to Exchange and then use POP3 to download mail and then read offline. Each of these protocols has an associated virtual server that administrators configure with IP addressing, a port numbering assignment, and authentication settings. See Table 8.1 for IP address and port-numbering information.

TABLE 8.1   Summary of Virtual Server IP Addresses and Port Assignments

Virtual Server / Protocol	Receiving IP Address	Sending IP Address	Default Port	Default Secure Port
SMTP	Any available IP address on the server	DNS MX record IP address for domain	25	465, Secure Sockets Layer (SSL) and Transport Layer Security (TLS)
IMAP4	Any available IP address on the server	IP address associated with the FQDN of the Exchange Server	143	993, Secure Sockets Layer (SSL)
POP3	Any available IP address on the server	IP address associated with the FQDN of the Exchange Server	110	995, Secure Sockets Layer (SSL)
HTTP	Any available IP address on the server	IP address associated with the FQDN of the Exchange Server	80	443, Secure Sockets Layer (SSL)

Note   The TCP port/IP address configuration must be unique on every virtual server. There can be multiple virtual servers sharing the same port, but not the same IP address.

Managing Virtual Servers

In general, managing the virtual server for one protocol is very similar to managing a virtual server for a different protocol. Administrative management of virtual servers include tasks such as enabling a virtual server, assigning ports, setting connection limits, starting or stopping a virtual server, and terminating connected users.

Virtual servers run as server processes and can be started, stopped, or paused. This is typically performed by administrators during maintenance or troubleshooting. Each method provides different administrative options. Stopping a virtual server halts all server connections and delivery of email messages both in and out of the server. When a virtual server is paused, all new incoming connections are stopped but current connections are kept alive. When an IMAP4 or POP3 virtual server is paused, active clients can still receive messages. When an SMTP virtual server is paused, no new connections are accepted, but existing queued messages can be delivered and new messages can be submitted to the queue for delivery. These messages will be delivered after the virtual server is restarted.

A master server process also exists for the SMTP, IMAP4, and POP3 virtual servers. This process halts all virtual servers using this process and stops delivery of messages for the service. When the master process is restarted, all associated virtual servers are restarted as well.

Starting, Stopping, and Pausing Virtual Servers

Use the following steps to start, stop, or pause a virtual server:

1. In ESM, if administrative groups are enabled, expand the administrative group you want to work with. Next, navigate to the Protocols container and expand the Servers node of the server you want to work with; then expand the Protocols node.

2. Expand the SMTP, IMAP4, or POP3 node and then right-click the virtual server you want to work with.

3. Choose Start to start the virtual server; choose Pause to pause it or Stop to stop it.

Stopping, starting, or pausing the master process is accomplished using the following steps:

1. Click Start, All Programs or Programs, Administrative Tools, and Computer Management.

2. Expand the Services and Applications node and then click Services. IMAP4, POP3, and SMTP are controlled by the Microsoft Exchange IMAP4, Microsoft Exchange POP3, and SMTP services.

3. In the right pane, scroll to and right-click the service to manage and then select Start, Stop, or Pause. The service can also be briefly stopped and started using the Restart command. If a service is paused, the service can be put back into operation by selecting the Resume command, as shown in Figure 8.1.

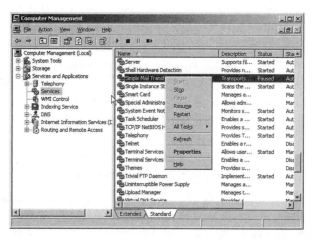

FIGURE 8.1   Using the Computer Management MMC to control the SMTP Master Process.

Changing Virtual Server Settings

Administrators may want to use alternative ports, IP settings, connection limits, and timeout values when configuring a virtual server. To change these settings, use the following steps:

1. In ESM, expand the administrative groups and then the administrative group you want to work with. In the left pane, navigate to the Protocols container. Expand Servers and then the server you want to work with.

2. Expand the Protocols node and then expand the protocol to work with—SMTP, IMAP4, or POP3. Right-click the protocol to administer and then select Properties.

3. On the General tab, use the drop-down box to select an available IP address. Select All Unassigned to allow the protocol to respond on all unassigned IP addresses configured for use on the server.

4. Click the Advanced button to display and configure the TCP port settings for the protocol. Port settings can be configured for all unassigned IP addresses or for individual IP addresses.

5. In the Advanced dialog box, modify the port settings by clicking one of the following options:

   • Add—Add a TCP port on an individual IP address basis or all unassigned IP address basis.

   • Edit—Edit the current Address list box selection's TCP port settings.

   • Remove—Remove the current Address list box selection's TCP port settings.

6. Click OK and then click OK again to complete the configuration changes.

Unless they are configured differently, virtual servers will accept an unlimited number of connections. In some situations, this may not be acceptable. Administrators may want to restrict incoming connections and set timeout limits for idle users. Modify the connection limits and timeout values using the following steps:

1. In ESM, expand the administrative groups and then the administrative group you want to work with. In the left pane, navigate to the Protocols container. Expand Servers and then the server to work with.

2. Expand the Protocols node and expand the protocol to work with—SMTP, IMAP4, or POP3. Right-click the protocol to administer it and then select Properties.

3. On the General tab, select the Limit Number of Connections To check box and then type in a limit value. To remove an existing connection limit, clear the Limit Number of Connections To check box.

4. The Connection Time Out field controls the connection timeout value. Type a timeout value in the field to define an acceptable idle time for connections.

 Tip Typically, the Connection Time Out value is set between 30 and 60 minutes. In most environments, 30 minutes is sufficient. If users are being disconnected during file downloads, increase this value to about 90 minutes. This should be sufficient for most file downloads.

Each time a user connects to a virtual server, a user session is created that lasts for the duration of the user's connection. Administrators can monitor user connections to check the server load and to monitor connection times. If necessary, administrators can terminate individual user sessions or all user sessions connected to a virtual server. To view or terminate user sessions, perform the following steps:

1. In ESM, expand the administrative groups and then the administrative group you want to work with. In the left pane, navigate to the Protocols container. expand Servers and then the server to work with.

2. Expand the Protocols node and then expand the protocol to work with—SMTP, IMAP4, or POP3. Double-click the virtual server to administer and then select the Current Sessions node to display a list of current sessions in the Details pane.

3. To end an individual user session, right-click a user in the Details pane and select Terminate. To end all user sessions, right-click any user in the Details pane and select Terminate All.

Administering POP3 Virtual Servers

POP3 servers are used to read mail on remote servers. Users log in and retrieve their mail via POP3 for offline use. A default POP3 virtual server is created during the Exchange installation. Additional POP3 virtual servers can be created using the following steps:

1. In ESM, expand the administrative groups and then the administrative group you want to work with. In the left pane, navigate to the Protocols container. Expand Servers, the server to work with, and then expand Protocols.

2. In the console tree, right-click POP3, choose New, and then select POP3 Virtual Server to start the server wizard. Type a descriptive name for the new POP3 server and click Next.

3. Using the drop-down list, select an available IP address. Choose All Unassigned so the POP3 server can respond on all configured but unassigned IP addresses on the server. The TCP port will be automatically assigned to port 110. Click Finish to complete the wizard.

Administering SMTP Virtual Servers

SMTP servers are used to handle mail submission and mail delivery; clients submit messages using SMTP, and servers use SMTP to transport messages. A default SMTP virtual server is created during the Exchange installation.

Creating SMTP Virtual Servers

Although one SMTP instance is sufficient for messaging needs, administrators can add additional SMTP virtual servers for fault tolerance. Additional SMTP virtual servers can be created using the following steps:

1. In ESM, expand the administrative groups and then the administrative group you want to work with. In the left pane, navigate to the Protocols container. Expand Servers, the server to work with, and then expand Protocols.

2. In the console tree, right-click SMTP, choose New, and then select SMTP Virtual Server to start the server wizard. Type a descriptive name for the new SMTP server and click Next.

3. Using the drop-down list, select an available IP address. Choose All Unassigned so the POP3 server can respond on all configured but unassigned IP addresses on the server. The TCP port will be automatically mapped to port 25. Click Finish to complete the wizard.

> **Tip** The default setting is for the SMTP virtual server to start automatically. If the server does not start automatically, check the TCP port/IP addresses settings to be sure the combination is not in conflict with another virtual server's settings. Use the SMTP virtual server's Properties page to resolve any conflicts.

Configuring Incoming Connections

Administrators may want to control incoming connections using different authentication methods. Exchange 2003 supports three authentication methods: anonymous, basic, and integrated Windows. Anonymous authentication allows users to access resources without providing user credential information. Basic authentication prompts for the user logon information without any encryption. If secure communications are configured on the server itself, basic authentication can be configured with SSL encryption. Integrated Windows authentication validates a user's identity using standard Windows security. When users log in to Windows, their credentials are encrypted and relayed to the SMTP server. As needed, administrators can modify the authentication methods using the following steps:

1. In ESM, expand the administrative groups and then the administrative group you want to work with. In the left pane, navigate to

the Protocols container. Expand Servers, the server to work with, and then expand Protocols.

2. Expand SMTP, right-click the virtual server to work with, and then select Properties. On the Access tab, click Authentication to display the Authentication dialog box as shown in Figure 8.2.

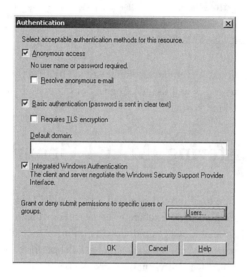

Figure 8.2   Using the Authentication dialog box to configure authentication methods for the SMTP virtual server.

3. Enable or disable anonymous logins by clicking the Anonymous Access check box. No user credentials will be necessary to access the SMTP virtual server.

4. Enable or disable basic authentication logins by clicking the Basic Authentication check box. The default domain field is empty by default. To ensure that clients authenticate properly, configure the default domain value field.

5. Enable or disable standard Windows logon security by clicking the Integrated Windows Authentication check box.

6. Click OK twice to complete the configuration changes.

Caution Enabling the option to resolve anonymous email may leave the Exchange organization suscepti- ble to email spoofing. Masquerading as an authorized user, hackers or other system users are provided the ability to send fake emails as if they are being sent by a legitimate user. Exercise caution when enabling this option.

Access to the virtual server can also be restricted by IP address, subnet, or domain. Administrators will use the Connections button on the Access tab to modify the default settings.

Administering IMAP4 Virtual Servers

IMAP4 servers are used to read mail and access public folders on remote servers. Clients log on to an Exchange server and download message headers and then read messages individually online. A default IMAP4 virtual server is created during the Exchange installation. If required for fault tolerance, additional IMAP4 virtual servers can be created using the following steps:

1. In ESM, expand the administrative groups and then the adminis- trative group you want to work with. In the left pane, navigate to the Protocols container. Expand Servers, the server to work with, and then expand Protocols.

2. In the console tree, right-click IMAP4, choose New, and then select IMAP4 Virtual Server to start the server wizard. Type a descriptive name for the new IMAP4 server and click Next.

3. Using the drop-down list, select an available IP address. Choose All Unassigned so the IMAP4 server can respond on all config- ured but unassigned IP addresses on the server. The TCP port will be automatically assigned to port 143. Click Finish to com- plete the wizard.

4. The new IMAP4 server should automatically start. If it doesn't, review the IP address/TCP port settings for any conflicts with other virtual server settings.

Administering HTTP Virtual Servers

HTTP servers allow authenticated users to access their mailboxes and public folder data. HTTP virtual servers can also be used to publish data to be accessed by offsite users or clients and provide access for Outlook Mobile Access or Exchange ActiveSync. When Exchange is installed, a default HTTP Virtual Server is created. As an organization grows, additional HTTP Virtual Servers may be needed for fault tolerance and load balancing. Create additional HTTP servers using the following steps:

1. In ESM, expand the administrative groups and then the administrative group you want to work with. In the left pane, navigate to the Protocols container; expand Servers, the server to work with, and then expand Protocols.

2. In the console tree, right-click HTTP, choose New, and then select HTTP Virtual Server. In the Properties dialog box, as shown in Figure 8.3, type a descriptive name for the new HTTP server in the Name field.

3. Using the drop-down list, select an available IP address. Choose All Unassigned to allow the HTTP server to respond on all configured but unassigned IP addresses on the server. The Transmission Control Protocol port will be automatically assigned to port 80 for HTTP and port 443 for SSL.

4. Click Advanced on the General tab. Use the Add, Remove, and Modify options to change the server's identity. To control the maximum number of simultaneous connections, select the Limit Number of Connections check box and then type in a limit.

5. If the default timeout value of 900 seconds is too long, type a new timeout value in the Time-Out (secs) field.

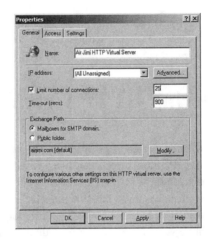

FIGURE 8.3   Using the Properties dialog box to create a new HTTP virtual server.

6. Determine whether the virtual server will provide access to mailboxes or public folders and then select Mailboxes for SMTP Domain or Public Folders. Click Modify to change the default settings.

7. Click OK to create the virtual server.

Summary

Virtual servers provide Exchange users with plenty of options for accessing mailboxes, public folders, and other resources. Access can come from within an organization or from outside the organization. With hundreds of settings and options, Exchange provides administrators the flexibility of configuring and securing Exchange to meet various organizational requirements.

LESSON 9

Securing Exchange with Policies and Permissions

This lesson delves into the basic security set up and management of recipient policies, system policies, permissions, and group security in Exchange 2003.

Managing Policies

In Exchange 2003, recipient policies and system policies are powerful administration tools. Policies enable administrators to create and specify management rules for Exchange recipients and Exchange server systems. Whereas recipient policies help administrators manage email addressing and mailbox messages, system policies help administrators manage servers and information stores.

Managing Recipient Policies

Administrators can use recipient policies to generate email addresses for users, groups, contacts, and other mail-enabled objects. The first recipient policy that an administrator creates will become the default recipient policy if one does not already exist in the organization. The default policy applies to all mail-enabled objects and establishes how default addresses are created for SMTP, X.400, and other gateways in the organization. The default policy is given the lowest priority; it is applied only when other recipient policies are not available. Although some settings, such as filters, cannot be changed on default policies, administrators can create new policies that are fully customizable. To create an email address recipient policy, use the following steps:

1. In ESM, expand the Recipients node and then select Recipient Policies. In the right pane, any available recipient policies will be displayed.

2. Right-click Recipient Policies, choose New, and then click Recipient Policy.

3. In the New Policy dialog box, select the Email Addresses check box and then click OK.

4. Type a descriptive name into the Name field. This makes it easy to know how and to what the policy applies.

5. Click the Modify button to show the Find Exchange Recipients dialog box. Select the recipient types to which to apply the new recipient policy by selecting the appropriate check boxes.

6. Using the Advanced Tab, set filters for the policy based on object type. To create a filter by department, click Field, point to User, and then select Department. Next, select a condition that meets organization objectives and then click Add to create the filter, as shown in Figure 9.1. Repeat this process to create additional filters.

FIGURE 9.1 Using the Advanced tab to configure filters on Exchange objects.

7. Click OK to finish defining filters and display the filter on the General tab. Use the Modify button to correct errors or make any changes.

8. Click OK to create the policy. The policy will be applied according to the schedule settings of the Recipient Update Service.

A policy is applied only once unless a policy is modified that causes Exchange to create new email addresses. You can create exceptions to recipient policies by waiting until the Recipient Update Service applies the policies and then completing the following steps:

1. In Active Directory Users and Computers, access the Recipient node containing the recipients to work with.

2. Double-click the recipient object to exclude from the recipient policy and then select the Email Addresses tab that is shown in the Properties dialog box.

3. From the Email Addresses tab, modify the settings for the selected recipient using one of the following options:

- Add a New Email Address—Click New. Select the type of email address in the New Email address dialog box and then click OK. Enter any requested info into the Properties box and click OK again.

- Modify an Existing Email Address—Highlight an email address, click Edit, and then change the email settings. Click OK to apply the modifications.

- Remove an Email Address—Highlight the email address to delete and then click Remove. Click Yes to confirm the deletion.

4. Click OK when all changes are completed. Repeat the preceding steps for other recipients that need policy exceptions.

The Recipient Update Service, which runs under the System Attendant, makes changes to email addresses based on changes to the recipient policies. The changes are made according to a specified schedule that is defined for the service. Administrators can view and/or modify the

Recipient Update Service interval. Use the following steps to change or modify the interval settings:

1. In ESM, expand the Recipients node by clicking the plus sign next to the Recipients node. Next, select Recipient Update Services.

2. In the right pane, available Recipient Update Services are displayed; one is for the enterprise configuration and one or more will be domains in the forest.

3. Right-click the service to work with and then select Properties. Use the Properties dialog box to view and modify the service's configuration settings. Within the Update Interval drop-down list, select an interval setting that best fits the organization's needs. If the predefined interval settings are not enough, use the Custom Schedule option and then click Customize to create a specialized interval schedule.

4. Click OK to apply the modifications.

Administrators may want to delete recipient policies that they have created. You can accomplish this by right-clicking the recipient policy, selecting Delete, and then confirming the deletion when prompted.

 Note   The default email address recipient policy is mandatory and cannot be deleted. Don't waste time right-clicking and looking for a Delete option; you won't find one!

Managing System Policies

System policies are a collection of configuration and control settings for servers and information stores. Exchange 2003 supports three types of system policies: mailbox store, public folder store, and server. System policies are configured through various property pages. Administrators will use the General properties page to configure server policies. To configure mailbox store policies, administrators will use the General,

Database, and Limits properties pages. Similarly, public store policies are configured using the General, Database, Replication, and Limits property pages.

Administrators will manage system policies differently from the way they manage recipient polices. Administrators are involved with the creation and implementation process, unlike recipient policies, which depend on the Recipient Update Service. Basically, administrators will first create a server, a public folder store, or a mailbox store policy. Next, administrators will specify the servers or stores to which the policy should apply by adding items to a policy. Then administrators will need to apply the policy to enforce it.

Administrators can create multiple policies of the same type, such as mailbox store policies, and apply the database, messaging, and replication policies to the same objects, the mailbox store. If two policies are conflicting, a notification will appear when the policy is being created and an administrator will have an opportunity to resolve the conflict. If the conflict is not resolved, the policy item in conflict will not be added.

You can create server policies using the following steps:

1. In ESM, beneath the Administrative Group node, click and expand the administrative group to work with. Right-click the System Policies node, point to New, and then select Server Policy.

 Note If the System Policies node does not exist, you will need to create one. Right-click the administrative group in which to create the policy, point to New, and then select System Policy Container.

2. In the New Policy dialog box, select the General check box and then click OK to display a Properties dialog box. Type a descriptive name for the policy.

3. On the General (Policy) tab, configure the server policy options, clicking the check boxes to enable the following options:

   • To log the message subject and make this subject visible when messages are tracked, select Enable Subject Logging and Display.

   • To track all messages that flow to and from the server, select Enable Message Tracking.

   • To remove all log files, select Remove Log Files. Configure the Remove Files Older Than (days) field to a value between 1 and 99; this text box specifies the maximum age that files can attain before automatic removal.

4. Click OK to complete creating the policy.

Any items inherited in the policy cannot be modified and will appear as disabled in the Server Properties dialog box.

After a policy is created, you will need to add items to the policy and apply the policy to the Exchange organization.

You can add items to the system policy using the following steps:

1. In ESM, under the Organization node or the Administrative node, access the System Policies node. Right-click the policy to work with and choose the appropriate item—Add Server, Add Public Folder Store, or Add Mailbox Store. The Select Item to Place Under the Control of This Policy dialog box will be displayed.

2. Select an item in the Name list box and then click Add. Repeat the step as necessary to place additional items under the policy. Click OK and then click Yes to confirm the addition of the item.

3. If the items are under the control of another policy, prompts will be displayed, asking to remove the items from the other policy's control. Click Yes to answer each prompt.

You can easily remove items from a system policy by completing the following steps:

1. In ESM, under the Organization node or the Administrative node, access the System Policies node and then double-click the policy to work with.

2. Items under control of the policy should be displayed in the right pane. Right-click the item to remove, select All Tasks, and then click Remove from Policy. Click Yes to confirm the item removal.

Administrators can modify a policy that is applied to one or more objects to change the properties on all the objects. Complete the following steps to modify a policy:

1. In ESM, under the Organization node or the Administrative node, access the System Policies node and then right-click the policy to modify. Click Properties and then use the tabs in the Properties dialog box to modify the policy.

2. Make the necessary modifications and then click OK to close the dialog box.

3. Right-click the policy, and then click Apply Now to apply the changes.

You can delete system policies by performing the following steps:

1. In ESM, under the Organization node or the Administrative node, access the System Policies node.

2. Right-click the policy to delete, point to Delete, and then click Delete.

 Tip Instead of deleting a policy, disable the policy by removing items within its control. This way the policy can be reapplied by adding items back into the policy rather than re-creating the entire policy from scratch.

Managing Permissions

In Active Directory, administrators manage security by using permissions. Contacts, users, and groups all have permissions assigned to them that control their access to resources in the organization. Permissions also control the actions that users, contacts, or groups can perform. Permissions can be applied directly to an object or they can be inherited: the default process by which the creation of an object causes the object (child) to assume the permissions of its parent object. For example, the root, or parent, of the server hierarchy is the Organization node. All other nodes (child nodes) in the tree inherit the Exchange permissions of Organization node. In itself, inheritance is an essential tool for simplifying the application of permissions and makes it possible (and simple) for permissions to be applied consistently in an object hierarchy.

Administrators often want to change the default permissions that are set by default when a child object inherits permissions from a parent object. Viewing security permissions for an Exchange server is accomplished by completing the following steps:

1. In ESM, right-click the root or top-level leaf node to work with.

2. Select Properties from the shortcut menu and then select the Security tab within the Properties dialog box, as shown in Figure 9.2.

 Note   The Properties option is not available on the shortcut menu of nonroot or nonleaf nodes such as Recipients or Server nodes. Try expanding the node and selecting a lower-level node. In addition, some nodes can be viewed and configured only using the Exchange Administration Delegation Wizard.

3. In the Group or User Names list box, select the object to view the permissions. The object permissions will be displayed in the Permissions list box; inherited permissions are displayed as shaded check boxes.

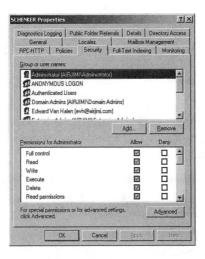

FIGURE 9.2   Using the Security tab to view and configure permissions on Exchange objects.

Setting Permissions

Administrators manage and control the use of Exchange server by setting permissions in various ways:

- Organizationwide—Administrators set permissions at the organization level and the permissions are applied through inheritance to all objects in the Exchange organization.

- Per server—Permissions are set on each server in the Exchange organization and the permissions are applied through inheritance to all child nodes on the server.

- Per storage group—Permissions are set at the storage group level and the permissions are applied through inheritance to all mailbox and public folder stores contained in the storage group.

- Per individual node—Permissions are set on an individual node.

Use the follow steps to configure Exchange server permissions:

1. In ESM, right-click the top-leaf or root-level node to work with. On the shortcut menu, select Properties and then click the Security tab in the Properties dialog box.

2. Groups or Users with access to the Exchange node will be listed in the Groups or User Names list box. Select a user or group to modify and then allow or deny them access permissions in the Permissions list box.

3. To set permissions for additional groups, users, or computers, click the Add button. Use the Select Users, Computers, or Groups dialog box to select users, computers, or groups to set access permissions.

4. In the Group or User Names list box, select the user, computer, or group to configure. Use the Permissions area to allow or deny permissions. Repeat as necessary.

5. Click OK to complete configuring permissions.

Delegating Permissions

Administrators may want to delegate control of the Exchange server without making a user a member of the Domain or Enterprise Administrators groups. An administrator may want to give his or her supervisor access to view the Exchange server settings but at the same time prevent the supervisor from modifying any settings. Exchange Administration Delegation Wizard (EADW) is the tool to use to delegate control of Exchange Server.

The level of permissions is determined by the level at which the wizard is started. If the Exchange Administration Delegation Wizard is started at the organization level, users or groups will have administrative permissions throughout the whole organization. If the Exchange Administration Delegation Wizard is started at the administrative group level, users or groups will have administrative permissions for that specific administrative group only. The Exchange Administration Delegation Wizard lets administrators configure the following administrative permissions:

- Exchange Full Administrator—Allows full administration of Exchange system information and modifying of permissions.

- Exchange Administrator—Allows full administration of Exchange system information, but users or groups cannot modify permissions.

- Exchange View Only Administrator—Allows only viewing of Exchange configuration information.

With Exchange Administration Delegation Wizard, you can set permissions using the following steps:

1. In ESM, right-click the organization or administrative groups to delegate control of; then click Delegate Control. This starts the Exchange Administration Delegation Wizard. Click Next to continue.

2. In the Users and Groups, click Add to grant a new user or group administrative permissions. In the Delegate Control dialog box, click Browse and then select the user or groups to delegate permissions to. Click OK to continue.

3. In the Delegate Control dialog box, use the Role drop-down box to select the appropriate role to delegate—Exchange Full Administrator, Exchange Administrator, or Exchange View Only Administrator—and then click OK. Repeat steps 2 and 3 to delegate additional permissions.

4. Click Next and then click Finish to complete permissions delegation.

Securing Groups

Administrators will want to secure the messaging environment by securing distribution and mail-enabled security groups. Exchange 2003 provides a simple way to configure messaging restrictions for a distribution group. Use the following steps to secure distribution groups so that only authenticated users are allowed access:

1. In Active Directory Users and Computers, right-click the distribution group to work with and select Properties.

2. Click the Exchange General tab. In the Message Restrictions section, click the From Authenticated Users Only check box.

3. Click OK when finished.

Administrators can add more restrictions to a group by allowing only a specific security group to access it. Use the following steps to restrict distribution group access to specific groups or users:

1. In Active Directory Users and Computers, right-click the distribution group to work with and select Properties.

2. Click the Exchange General tab. In the Message Restrictions section, click the Only From option button.

3. Click Add and enter the security group that has permission to send messages to the distribution group. Click OK and then click OK again to finish.

Using Microsoft Baseline Security Analyzer

Microsoft Baseline Security Analyzer (MBSA) v. 2.0 is a tool that identifies common security misconfigurations and missing security updates (hot fixes) on computer systems. MBSA includes a GUI and Command Line Interface (CLI) that administrators can use to scan local or remote Windows systems and that provides security recommendations and specific remediation guidance. Get MBSA from Microsoft at http://www.microsoft.com/technet/security/tools/mbsahome.mspx.

After MBSA is downloaded and installed, use the following steps to run a local or remote system scan:

1. From the Start, All Programs menu, click Microsoft Baseline Security Analyzer 2.0. At the welcome screen, select one of the scanning options to scan a single computer, multiple computers, or view existing security reports.

2. Configure computer and scanning options. If you're unsure, use the default settings. Click Start Scan to commence security scanning.

3. Review the scan report details screen as shown in Figure 9.3. Security issues are categorized in various levels: a red X indicates a critical issue, a yellow X indicates a noncritical issue, a green check mark indicates a passed test with no issues, and a blue asterisk indicates a best practice. For easier reading, administrators can print out a hard copy of the report using the print option on the left side of the screen.

4. Update security vulnerabilities as necessary.

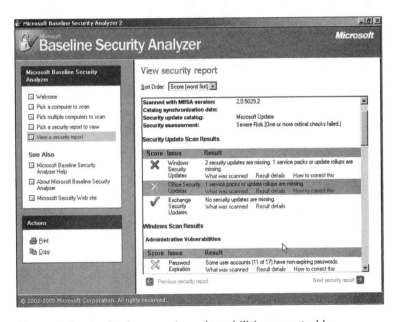

FIGURE 9.3 Reviewing security vulnerabilities reported by Microsoft Baseline Security Analyzer.

Summary

Exchange 2003 provides many ways to implement server security. Administrators should assess the messaging environment's risks, establish security policies and permissions, and implement a standardized security plan that promotes a secure messaging environment for their organization.

LESSON 10

Managing Outlook Web Access (OWA) and Outlook Mobile Access (OMA)

This lesson delves into the basic setup and management of Outlook Web Access and Outlook Mobile Access in Exchange 2003.

Introducing OWA for Exchange Server 2003

Outlook Web Access (OWA) is an Exchange email client technology that lets users access their mailboxes and public folder data using a Web browser and standard Internet protocols, such as HTTP and an HTTP extension, Web Distributed Authoring and Versioning (WebDAV). When users access mailboxes and public folders over the intranet or Internet, an HTTP virtual server hosted by Exchange 2003 is working behind the scenes to grant access and deliver files to the browser.

OWA and a default HTTP virtual server are automatically installed and configured for use when administrators install Exchange 2003. Although ports may need to be opened on the firewall to allow users access to their mailboxes and public folder data, administrators need to provide the Uniform Resource Locator (URL) for the users to put in their browser's address field.

Note This lesson is written assuming the email client is accessing OWA in Premium mode. The Basic mode experience may differ from explanations in this lesson.

Using OWA

Optimized for screen resolutions of 800×600 or higher, OWA supports two type of user modes when accessed with Internet Explorer 5 or later or Netscape Navigator 4.7 or later: Basic mode and Premium mode. Premium mode provides a feature-rich experience close to Microsoft's Office Outlook 2003, including drag-and-drop capability, right-click access to shortcut menus, and an expandable folder hierarchy. Spell check, the Reading/Preview pane, server-side rules, and forms-based authentication are a few of the other enhancements featured in OWA.

As shown in Figure 10.1, the Premium view is what most users will automatically experience when using Internet Explorer 5 and later. If users cannot right-click and access shortcut menus, either they are using an old browser version or the technology set necessary for a rich experience has been disabled. Premium mode is more bandwidth intensive than Basic mode, so be sure this is taken into account during planning phases. Basic mode is useful for clients using slow dial-up connections; this mode still allows them basic email capability with the bells and whistles of Premium mode.

OWA contains a feature set that enhances the user interface, user productivity, user security, and gives increased performance. User-interface enhancements include a forms-based login screen, new themes and colors, context menus, a reading pane, and keyboard shortcuts. User productivity enhancements include calendaring improvements, Search Folders, message signature, Personal Tasks, and spell checking. User security enhancements include attachment and web-beaconing clocking and privacy protection.

Many of the enhancements have configurable settings that help users to manage their inbox, calendar, contacts, tasks, public folders, and mailboxes in OWA. By clicking the Options shortcut in the Task pane, users can modify OWA settings and then apply the changes by clicking Save and Close. The Options page contains such settings items as the out-of-office assistant, the spelling check, email security, and junk email protection.

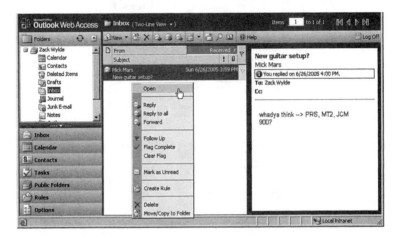

FIGURE 10.1 The Premium mode of OWA has most of the features of Outlook 2003.

Managing OWA

By default, Exchange 2003 enables OWA for users. Without any administrative intervention, internal and external users can access their mailboxes and public folder data. If necessary, administrators can disable OWA for individual users using the following steps:

1. Open Active Directory Users and Computers.

2. In the toolbar, choose View Menu and then select Advanced Features. This enables the Advanced Features for viewing and configuration.

3. Double-click the user account you want to work with. This opens the Properties dialog box for the user account.

4. Click the Exchange Features tab to display the OWA and mobile access features as shown in Figure 10.2.

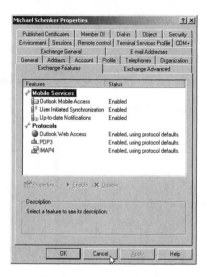

FIGURE 10.2   Using the Exchange Features tab to view and config-ure Outlook Web Access settings.

5. Under Protocols, select Outlook Web Access and then click Disable or Enable as appropriate.

6. Click OK when finished.

WebDAV is used to access mailboxes and public folders over the Internet or the company intranet. WebDAV allows email clients to access mail-boxes with only a browser and a URL. Clients type the provided URL into the address field of the browser and then enter their username and password. For example, to access the mailbox for the Exchange alias mschenker, type **http://{servername}/exchange**, where {servername} is the placeholder name for the HTTP virtual server hosted by the Exchange server. When prompted, type the username **mschenker** and the mailbox password.

Similarly, WebDAV allows access to the default folder tree. When users have access after they have logged in to the mailbox, they can click the Public Folders tab. Alternatively, the folder's URL can be typed into the browser's address field to gain public folder access. To access the public folder tree, type **http://{servername}/public**, where {servername} is the placeholder name for the HTTP virtual server hosted by the Exchange server and public is the default name of the Public Folders web share. Users can also access alternative public folder trees. In this example, a user can access an alternative public folder called guitarists by typing **http://{servername}/guitarists** into the browser address field, where {servername} is the placeholder name for the HTTP virtual server hosted by the Exchange server and guitarist is the default name of the alternative public folder tree.

Caution   If users see an error page when performing the preceding tasks, they typically have not been authenticated and granted access to the Exchange information. When troubleshooting mailbox and public folder access problems, administrators should make sure that users have proper logon and access permissions before making configuration changes.

Introducing OMA for Exchange Server 2003

Originally in Mobile Information Server 2002, Outlook Mobile Access (OMA) has been enhanced in Exchange Server 2003. Using a broad-reach wireless device that includes web-browser capability such as PDA, Smartphone, or Pocket PC, users can take advantage of Microsoft's latest mobile device solution. OMA generates the following markup languages for display on supported devices:

- HTML
- xHTML and WAP 2.x
- cHTML and iMode

Unsupported devices can also be used with Outlook Mobile Access; however, the experience will not be fully comparable to the rich feature set of supported devices.

 Note   Wireless Markup Language (WML) is also generated by OMA. However, Microsoft has not tested WML for all devices and gateway configurations and does not support WML. Information regarding currently supported devices can be found at http://support.microsoft.com/default.aspx?scid=kb;en-us;821835. New devices are supported through a Device Update pack. An updated Device Update package is available for download from Microsoft every six months.

Using OMA and supported devices, users can access the following messaging and collaboration features:

- Email—Includes Read, Reply, Forward, Delete, or Flag messages, message composition, and folder navigation.

- Calendar—Includes Accept, Decline, or Tentative meeting requests; compose and edit appointments with attendees support.

- Contacts—View, Create, or Edit personal contacts, search personal and global address list contacts, and save GAL contacts to personal and email contacts.

- Tasks—View, Create, and Edit tasks.

Setting Up OMA

Outlook Mobile Access is installed by default when administrators initially install Exchange 2003. Although OMA is installed and users are enabled for mobile access, OMA is disabled globally. After access is enabled, users point their mobile devices toward the OMA server through a URL, such as **http://{servername}/oma**, where {servername} is the server name of the OMA server. Unlike Microsoft Outlook Web Access, however, you cannot specify a specific user account in the URL because Outlook Mobile Access adds a unique identifier to the URL as part of session state management.

> **Caution**   Although not required, a front-end server is typically recommended. Using OMA directly against a back-end server may cause conflicts with Outlook Web Access and Forms Based Authentication or if SSL is required for the Exchange virtual directory in Internet Information Server (IIS). If SSL or Forms Based Authentication is required, administrators will need to create a new OMA virtual directory. For help, see Microsoft Knowledgebase article 817379. For related information, see Microsoft Knowledgebase article 817317.

Setting up OMA is a quick and easy process using Exchange System Manager. To enable OMA, use the following steps:

1. In ESM, navigate to and expand the Global Settings node. Right-click the Mobile Services and select Properties to display the Mobile Services Properties dialog box shown in Figure 10.3.

2. On the General tab, click the check box next to Enable Outlook Mobile Access.

3. To enable unsupported devices, click the check box next to Enable Unsupported Devices.

4. Click OK to finish.

After OMA is enabled, administrators can test the setup by pointing a web browser to a URL, such as **http://{servername}/oma**, where {servername} is the name for the OMA server. If the server is operating properly, a simple page will be displayed as shown in Figure 10.4.

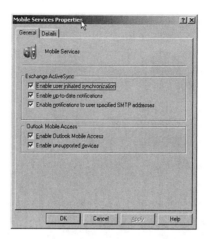

FIGURE 10.3 Enabling Outlook Mobile Access via the Mobile Services Properties dialog box.

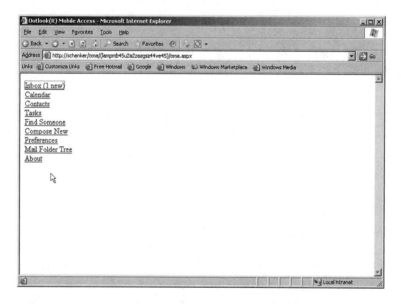

FIGURE 10.4 Using Internet Explorer to test basic operation of Outlook Mobile Access.

After basic testing with a browser is complete, administrators can test with mobile device emulators for devices, such as the Pocket PC SDK or the Openwave Mobile SDK, or test with actual supported devices that will be used in their organization for access to OMA.

Testing Exchange access with a mobile device is a multistep process. First, users must have Internet access through a wireless carrier. Then the users initiate the device's browser and point the browser to the Outlook Mobile Access URL. Users authenticate to Exchange using their username, password, and domain information.

On a Pocket PC, the step-by-step process is the following:

1. Configure the mobile device to use the wireless carrier's Internet service. On the Today screen, tap Start, and then tap Internet Explorer to display the Internet Explorer Screen.

2. Tap View and then tap Address Bar.

3. Tap the address bar and then type in the Outlook Mobile Access URL, such as **http://exchange.airjimi.com/oma**.

4. Enter username, password, and domain information when prompted.

After authentication, users have access to their inbox, calendar, contacts, or tasks and can configure search options or change user preferences.

Managing OMA

Administrators may want to change and modify Outlook Mobile Access settings. To change mobile access settings for users, use the following steps:

1. In Active Directory Users and Computers, expand the domain, and then open the node for the user setting to work with.

2. Right-click the user or users (hold down the Ctrl key and left-click to select multiple users) whose OMA settings are to be modified, and then select Exchange Tasks. At the Welcome page, click Next to continue.

3. In Exchange Task Wizard, on the Available Tasks page in the Select a Task to Perform section, choose Configure Exchange Features, and then click Next.

4. On the Configure Exchange Features page, select Outlook Mobile Access, and then select one of the following:

   • Select Enable to allow users to use Outlook Mobile Access.

   • Select Disable to prevent users from using Outlook Mobile Access.

   • Select Do Not Modify to prevent the users' settings from being modified when more than one user has been selected.

5. Click Next to apply modifications and display the Exchange Task Wizard summary page as shown in Figure 10.5.

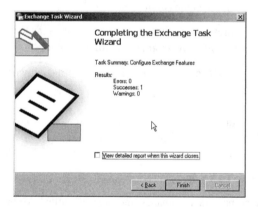

FIGURE 10.5   Viewing the Exchange Task Wizard summary screen after modifying Outlook Mobile Access settings.

6. To see a detailed report as shown in Figure 10.6, click the check box next to View Detailed Report When This Wizard Closes and click Finish.

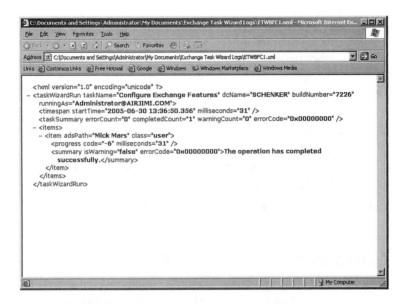

```
C:\Documents and Settings\Administrator\My Documents\Exchange Task Wizard Logs\ETWBFC1.xml - Microsoft Internet Ex...
File   Edit   View   Favorites   Tools   Help
Back        search   Favorites
Address   C:\Documents and Settings\Administrator\My Documents\Exchange Task Wizard Logs\ETWBFC1.xml                   Go
Links   Customize Links   Free Hotmail   Google   Windows   Windows Marketplace   Windows Media

    <?xml version="1.0" encoding="unicode" ?>
  - <taskWizardRun taskName="Configure Exchange Features" dcName="SCHENKER" buildNumber="7226"
      runningAs="Administrator@AIRJIMI.COM">
      <timespan startTime="2005-06-30 13:36:50.356" milliseconds="31" />
      <taskSummary errorCount="0" completedCount="1" warningCount="0" errorCode="0x00000000" />
    - <items>
      - <item adsPath="Mick Mars" class="user">
          <progress code="-6" milliseconds="31" />
          <summary isWarning="false" errorCode="0x00000000">The operation has completed
          successfully.</summary>
        </item>
      </items>
    </taskWizardRun>
```

FIGURE 10.6   Viewing the Exchange Task Wizard Detailed report via Internet Explorer.

Exchange 2003 enables mobile services for each user by default. Administrators can manage mobile services for individual users. Using the following steps, administrators can disable or enable mobile access:

1. Start Active Directory Users and Computers.

2. Select Advanced Features from the toolbar View Menu. Advanced Features will now be enabled for administrator view and configuration.

3. In Active Directory Users and Computers, double-click the username you want to work with and open the Properties dialog box for the user account.

4. Click the Exchange Features tab.

5. Under the Mobile Services section, select Outlook Mobile Access and then click Enable or Disable, as appropriate. Disabling mobile services will prevent users from synchronizing or browsing with Exchange.

6. Under the Mobile Services Section, select User Initiated Synchronization and then click Enable or Disable, as appropriate. Disabling synchronization prevents a user from receiving or sending synchronization requests, but still allows wireless browsing access.

7. Under the Mobile Services Section, select Up-to-Date Notifications and then click Enable or Disable, as appropriate. Disabling Up-to-Date Notifications prevents Exchange from notifying the user when new messages are received and also disables background synchronization.

8. Click OK when finished.

Summary

Keeping pace with today's variety of evolving workplace environments, networking technologies, and changing ways in which people work, communicate, and collaborate, Exchange 2003 has been improved to provide an enhanced user interface while maintaining support for a variety of messaging protocols and client interfaces. Outlook Web Access provides a GUI and feature set that rivals the look and feel of Microsoft Office Outlook 2003. Outlook Mobile access technologies provide mobile, roaming users a similar experience through wireless mobile devices.

LESSON 11

Managing and Using Microsoft Office Outlook 2003

This lesson delves into the new and improved feature set and basic configuration of Microsoft Outlook 2003 management in Exchange 2003.

Introducing the New Features in Microsoft Office Outlook 2003

Communication means have changed over the years. People used to communicate with each other primarily by phone and mail correspondence. Computer and high technology have changed the ways people communicate at work. Exchange 2003 encompasses the new communication paths and provides the capability to access corporate email from different types of networks, computers, and handheld devices in different locations, including at home, at work, and on the road.

Outlook 2003 and Exchange 2003 have been improved to provide a rich experience to users no matter how they are connected. Prior versions of Outlook and Exchange were optimized for LAN use, where networks are typically fast and reliable. When the network was fast and responsive, the quality of the user experience was great; when the network was slow and unresponsive, the quality of the user experience suffered. The latest combination of Exchange 2003 and Outlook 2003 fulfills the goal of a consistent user experience with rich support for calendaring and email management and includes new features such as Exchange Cached mode, Remote Procedure Call (RPC) over HTTP, enhanced security, antispam, and mail filtering and blocking.

Outlook 2003 is the most common Exchange client in use in corporate environments. The introduction of RPC over HTTP removes the need for Virtual Private Network (VPN) access to Exchange over the Internet. Because of this additional technology, Outlook is a great option for remote and offsite users. One caveat is that RPC over HTTP requires Exchange 2003 to be running on top of Windows Server 2003.

Configuring Outlook 2003

Administrators can install Outlook 2003 as a standalone product or as part of Office 2003. If an email application such as Outlook Express already exists on the computer, administrators can choose whether to upgrade the email application. Upgrading the application allows importing of existing email messages, contacts, and other information into Outlook 2003. This provides an opportunity to ease the transition to the new email client by eliminating a manual transfer of existing information. The other option is to not upgrade the existing client and instead perform a new email client installation. In that case, there is no option to import existing mail, contacts, or data. This data will be available only in the previously configured email program.

If no other email application is installed on the computer, the import option will not be available, and administrators will be prompted to configure Outlook to use one of the following options:

- Microsoft Exchange Server—Connect directly to Exchange Server. This option is best suited for users on the local area network. If users are planning to connect to Exchange Server via RTP over HTTP, they will also use this option.

- POP3—Connect to Exchange Server or Post Office Protocol 3 (POP3) email server via the Internet. This option is best suited for remote office or home users using broadband or dial-up Internet connections. Email can be downloaded, but mailbox folders cannot be synchronized.

- IMAP—Connect to Exchange Server or Internet Message Access Protocol (IMAP) email server via the Internet. This option is best suited for remote office or home users using broadband or dial-up Internet connections. Email can be down-loaded and mailbox folders can also be synchronized.

- HTTP—Connect to an HTTP email server, such as Hotmail, Yahoo, or Gmail, via the Internet. This option is best suited as an alternative email configuration option. Users can have access to a web-based email service and still have access to a corporate email server.

- Additional Server Types—Connect to a third-party email server. This option is typically used in addition to a configured Exchange Server connection.

Initial Configuration: Setting Up Outlook to Connect to Exchange Server

During the installation of Outlook as a standalone product or the first time that administrators run Outlook after installing it via Office 2003, a prompt to configure Outlook with Exchange Server or other Internet email servers will be displayed. Use the following steps to configure Outlook to connect to an Exchange Server:

1. When prompted, click Yes to configure Outlook to connect to Exchange Server or other Internet email servers.

2. As shown in Figure 11.1, select Microsoft Exchange Server as the server type to use with Outlook, and then click Next.

3. Type the hostname of the mail server into the Microsoft Exchange Server field. The name can be entered as a simple name, such as XMAIL, or as the fully qualified domain name (FQDN) of the mail server, such as mail.pandoranetworks.com. Using a FQDN helps ensure a connection in case the mail server is located in a different domain or forest.

4. Type the user's domain logon name or domain username, such as Walker or James Walker. Verify that the name entered is the correct username for the mailbox by clicking Check Name.

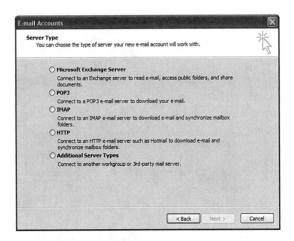

FIGURE 11.1   Selecting the server type to install with Outlook 2003.

5. Typically, administrators will want to store a local copy of the user's email on the user's computer. If so, click Next to continue. If the computer is a shared computer or has limited hard disk space, administrators may not want to store a local copy of the user's email on the computer. If that is the case, clear the Use Local Copy of Mailbox check box and then click Next.

6. Click Finish to complete the configuration of Outlook. Outlook will generate a Welcome message for the user.

Initial Configuration: Setting Up Outlook to Connect to Internet Mail or Other Server Types

Use the following steps to configure Outlook to connect to Internet mail or other server types:

1. When prompted, click Yes to configure Outlook to connect to an Exchange server, Internet email server, or other email server type.

2. Select the Internet email server type to use with Outlook—POP3, IMAP, HTTP—and then click Next.

3. In the User Information section, type in a username that will appear in the From field of outgoing messages of this user, such as James Walker, and then type the email address of the user, such as walker@pandoranetworks.com.

4. In the Logon Information section, type the user's logon name and password. For IMAP and POP3 servers, the information should be in the form of domain\email_alias, such as pandora\walker. Some instances may take the form of domain/email_alias, such as pandora/walker.

5. If POP3 or IMAP is selected, type the FQDN for the incoming and outgoing mail servers. These entries may or may not be the same; some organizations have different incoming and outgoing servers. Gather this information ahead of time to ensure a smooth configuration.

6. If HTTP is selected, the HTTP mail service can be selected as Hotmail, MSN, or Other. If Other is chosen, administrators must provide the URL to the main page of the HTTP service, such as http://mail.gmail.com.

7. For added security, administrators may select Log On Using Secure Password Authentication (SPA). This option ensures that some type of encryption is used and passwords are not sent over the Internet in clear-text format.

8. Check the POP3 account settings by clicking Test Account Settings. If the configuration is correct, all tests will pass and Outlook will successfully send a test email message.

9. Click Close, Next, and Finish to complete the Outlook configuration.

The Outlook client is now ready for use.

Using Outlook 2003

End users might not notice many enhancements or changes made to Outlook, but they'll be sure to notice the new graphical user interface, which includes a number of additional usability and productivity features. Outlook 2003 also resolves issues with email management, security, and communication that existed in previous versions of Outlook

New User Interface

The new graphical interface, shown in Figure 11.2, enhances the user experience with Outlook 2003. The Outlook bar and Folder list in previous versions of Outlook have been merged to form the new Navigation pane, which includes eight standard modules (Mail, Calendar, Contacts, Journal, and so on).

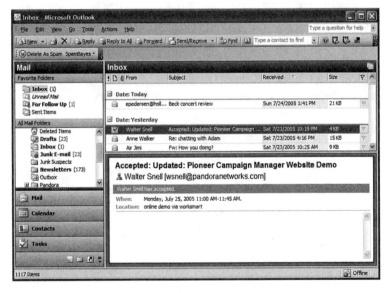

FIGURE 11.2 Exploring the new graphical user interface of Outlook 2003.

The Navigation pane, located on the left side of the Outlook interface, changes according to which module is selected and can be resized to maximize "real estate" in Outlook. If a user selects the Mail module, all the user's Mail folders will be displayed, including the Exchange Mailbox, any personal folders, or any other mailboxes the user has access to. Similarly, if a user selects the Calendar module, the user's Calendar will be displayed; a new enhancement allows the capability to see multiple calendars side-by–side, with each calendar shown in a different color.

The new interface also includes a Reading pane, which replaces the Preview pane in previous versions of Outlook. The Reading pane can be placed at the bottom or to the right of the email message list. It can also be toggled on or off.

Managing Email

Outlook 2003 helps users effectively manage email messages. New management features target the high volume of daily messages that plague many users. To help organize and prioritize messages, Outlook includes the following features: a desktop notification pop-up alert near the taskbar that indicates a received email, flagging of messages with different colors, automatic grouping of email messages (the old current view settings are still there as well, just hidden away on the View, Arrange By menu), and Search folders for searching messages based on specific criteria.

Outlook also includes antispam features designed to block unwanted junk mails. Four levels of protection range from no protection at all to safe lists only, where only messages from people or domains specified by the user are allowed through. Email messages can also be filtered by user-specified lists of Safe Senders (individual trusted email addresses or contacts), Safe Recipients (individual trusted email addresses that won't be considered junk mail), and Blocked Senders (addresses or domains considered junk mailers). Each of these lists includes an import/export utility so they can be shared among Outlook users.

Connecting and Caching

Previous versions of Outlook had performance issues. If the network was slow, connecting and synchronizing to Exchange was painfully slow. If the Exchange server was not available, users had no method to continue working. Outlook changes that with new connection modes that accommodate fast or slow network conditions. When using a fast connection with a direct connection to Exchange, Outlook copies the entire email message (header, body, and attachments). When using a slow connection, Outlook retrieves only the message headers. Outlook automatically determines the best connection speed for network conditions.

Outlook 2003 also uses caching to improve performance. Outlook can work in a cached mode where a constant connection to Exchange is not required. In cached mode, Outlook downloads and retrieves an initial copy of a user's mailbox and address book. If the Exchange Server is not available, a user can continue to work until a connection is established.

Introducing RPC over HTTP for Outlook 2003

Administrators can configure user accounts in Outlook 2003 to connect to Microsoft Exchange Server 2003 over the Internet without the need to use virtual private network connections. This feature—connecting to an Exchange account by using Remote Procedure Call (RPC) over HTTP—allows Outlook users to securely access their Exchange Server accounts from the Internet when they are traveling or working outside their organization's firewall from a home office or remote office. Users do not need any special connections or hardware such as smart cards and security tokens to access their Exchange accounts. Eliminating the complexity of virtual private networks, RPC over HTTP simplifies secure access to Exchange 2003.

Configuring RPC over HTTP

RPC over HTTP requires several components for proper operation on both client and server systems. Client workstations need to have Microsoft Windows XP with Service Pack 1 and the Q331320 hot fix (or a later service pack) and Outlook 2003 installed on the workstation. Server requirements are Microsoft Windows Server 2003 on global catalog servers, and RPC proxy servers and Exchange 2003 on all front-end and back-end servers. After the prerequisites are met, the servers and clients can be configured for RPC over HTTP access.

Configuring Exchange Server for RPC over HTTP

RPC over HTTP requires the Exchange Server to support HTTP proxy.
Two items must be configured on the Exchange Server to support the
remote connection:

- Install the RPC over HTTP Proxy service

- Configure IIS to support RPC over HTTP

Installing the RPC over HTTP Proxy service is accomplished using the
following steps:

1. Log on to the Exchange Server using an account with local
   administrative privileges.

2. From the Start menu, launch the Windows Control Panel applet
   and then select Add or Remove Programs. Click Add/Remove
   Windows Components.

3. Select the Network Services component and then click Details to
   display the Networking Services dialog box, as shown in
   Figure 11.3.

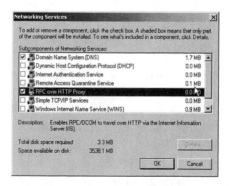

FIGURE 11.3   Selecting the RPC over HTTP Proxy Windows
component.

4. Check the box for RPC over HTTP and then click OK.

5. Click Next to install the RPC over HTTP proxy component. The Windows 2003 server media may need to be inserted during this process.

After the RPC over HTTP component is installed, reboot the Exchange Server in preparation for configuring IIS authentication settings. After the server has restarted, use the following steps to configure the RPC virtual directory for Basic authentication:

1. Log on to the Exchange server using an account with local administrative privileges.

2. From the Start menu, select All Programs or Programs, Administrative Tools, and then launch Internet Information Services Manager.

3. In the left pane, expand the Server, expand Web Sites, and then expand the Default website. Right-click the RPC Virtual Directory container and select Properties.

4. In the RPC Properties dialog box, select the Directory Security tab. Under the Authentication and access control section, click Edit. Deselect the Enable Anonymous Authentication and select the Basic Authentication option by clicking the check box (Integrated Windows Authentication should also be selected by default). Then click OK.

5. On the RPC Properties page, click Edit under the Secure communications section. Select Require Secure Channel (SSL) and Require 128-Bit Encryption by clicking both check boxes. Click OK to save changes and then click OK once more to exit the RPC Properties dialog box.

Configuring Outlook 2003 for RPC over HTTP

After the server components are configured, Outlook must be configured for RPC over HTTP by setting options on the user's Outlook Profile. The Outlook client can be configured to use RPC over HTTP whether or not Outlook has access to Exchange. This allows remote users to configure their Outlook without first having a VPN connection established to their internal network.

 Tip When configured for RPC over HTTP in an offline mode, the Outlook client may appear to hang up. Don't be alarmed; after a 30 second or so timeout, configuration changes will be able to be completed.

Administrators can configure Outlook 2003 to use RPC over HTTP by performing the following steps on an existing Outlook Profile:

1. From the Start menu, launch the Windows Control Panel applet and then select the Mail icon by double-clicking it.

2. In the Mail Setup dialog box, click the Email Accounts button. Verify that the View or Change Existing Email Accounts option button is selected, and then click Next to continue.

3. The list of email accounts appears. Select the Exchange server account and then click the Change button.

4. On the Exchange Server settings dialog screen, click the More Settings button to display the Microsoft Exchange Server Properties page.

5. Select the Connections tab. In the Exchange over the Internet section, enable the check box next to Connect to My Exchange Mailbox Using HTTP. Click the Exchange Proxy Settings button. The Exchange Proxy Settings dialog box will appear as shown in Figure 11.4.

6. In the Use This URL to Connect to My Proxy Server for Exchange field, enter the FQDN for the RPC proxy server. Enable the check boxes for the Connect Using SSL Only and Mutually Authenticate the Session When Connecting with SSL options. Also enter the FQDN of the RPC proxy server in the Principal Name for Proxy Server box. Be sure to use a format of msstd:FQDN of RPC Proxy Server (for example, msstd:mail.pandornetworks.com).

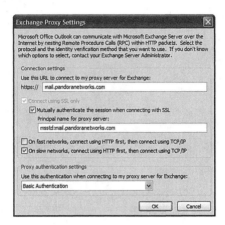

FIGURE 11.4   Configuring the Exchange Proxy Settings.

7. Because the RPC Virtual server is configured for Basic Authentication, change the value for the Use This Authentication When Connecting to My Proxy Server for Exchange drop-down list option to Basic Authentication.

8. Click OK to save the changes and then click OK to exit the Microsoft Exchange Server dialog box.

9. On the Exchange Server Settings screen, click Next.

10. On the Email Accounts dialog box, click Finish to exit, and then click Close to exit the Mail Setup dialog box.

The Outlook client is now configured for RPC over HTTP.

Tip Outlook 2003 can be configured to connect to an Exchange server by default using RPC over HTTP. To enable this option on the Exchange Proxy Settings dialog screen, select the check box next to On Fast Networks, Connect to Exchange Using HTTP First, Then Connect Using TCP/IP. A fast network has bandwidth greater than 128 kilobits per second (Kbps). A slow network has bandwidth that is less than or equal to 128Kbps.

Using Outlook 2003 via RPC over HTTP

Users will notice minimal functional difference when using RPC over HTTP with their Outlook email client. In most cases, except for easier access when offsite or in a remote office, users may not even know that Outlook is configured for this feature. To test whether Outlook is using HTTP, administrators and/or power users can use the following steps to verify that Outlook connects to the Exchange computer using RPC over HTTP:

1. On the Start menu, click Run, type `outlook /rpcdiag`, and then click OK.

2. Type the user credentials into the Username and Password boxes, and then click OK.

3. If HTTPS appears in the Conn column in the Exchange Server Connection Status dialog box, Outlook is connected by using RPC over HTTP. Otherwise, recheck the client setup and the server setup to make sure no configuration steps were missed.

 Tip Testing can also be accomplished while Outlook is running. In Outlook, press the Ctrl key while right-clicking the Outlook icon in the system tray. An additional option, Connection Status, will appear on the context menu. Click Connection Status to display the Exchange Server Connection Status dialog box.

Summary

Outlook 2003 is a full-featured email client that onsite, offsite, and mobile users can use. With full support of the latest messaging features, such as its sleek graphical interface, RTP over HTTP, Cached mode Connections, antispam and mail filtering, Outlook offers rich support for calendaring, scheduling, and email management—all the bells and whistles that workgroup and corporate users need.

LESSON 12

Performance Monitoring, Optimizing, and Troubleshooting

This lesson delves into the tools and methods for monitoring, optimizing, and troubleshooting performance of Exchange 2003.

Message Tracking and Logging

Message tracking helps administrators monitor the flow of messages out of and into the organization. Because public folder posts are handled similar to email messages, message tracking can also help monitor public folder usage. When message tracking is enabled, Exchange maintains daily logs of messages transported within the organization. Logs are useful for figuring out the status of a message, such as sent, received, or waiting in the queue for delivery. Logs are also useful for troubleshooting delivery and routing problems.

Tracking Messages

Different message-logging settings can be configured on Exchange servers within the organization. Standard message tracking allows searches for messages by date, time, message ID, sender, or recipient. Extended message tracking allows the same search criteria as standard message tracking, in addition to subject-line information and the capability to search messages based on message state—All Messages, Frozen, and Retry. Use the following steps to configure message logging:

1. In ESM, expand the administrative group that contains the server you want to work with. Expand Servers and then right-click the server and select Properties. The server's Properties dialog box will display as shown in Figure 12.1.

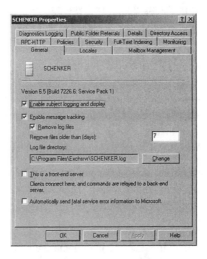

FIGURE 12.1   Configuring message tracking using the server's Properties dialog box.

2. Select the Enable Message Tracking check box to enable standard logging and message tracking. When prompted, write down the path to the network share noted in the pop-up dialog box; administrators will need to grant read access to the network share for users who will perform message tracking.

Note If the Enable Message Tracking check box is grayed out, check the server policy object applied to the server; most likely the server is part of a server policy. To resolve, administrators must either enable message tracking on the policy or remove the server from this policy.

3. Select the Enable Subject Logging and Display check box and then select the Enable Message Tracking check box to enable extended logging and tracking features.

4. To periodically delete log files, select the Remove Log Files check box. Type a logging interval value between 1 and 99 in the Remove Files Older Than (days) Field. Typically, log files should be kept at least seven days.

5. Click OK to complete the configuration.

Administrators can now search through the message-tracking logs by specifying the message id, sender, recipient, date, or the message, and also specify the server that processed the messages. The search is performed using the Message Tracking Center and the following steps:

1. In ESM, navigate the console tree in the left pane and expand the Tools node by double-clicking. Then select Message Tracking Center.

2. Enter the appropriate search criteria (message id, sender or recipient email address, server name) and then click Find Now to begin the search. Messages matching the criteria will be displayed. Click Stop to cancel message searching.

3. Select a message to display its message tracking history.

 Caution Message-tracking logs can grow large on servers processing many inbound and outbound messages. Be sure adequate hard disk space is available for tracking log files.

Logging Virtual Servers and Diagnostics Logging

Protocol logging allows administrators to track commands sent to virtual servers from client machines. It can be used to help troubleshoot problems with SMTP, HTTP, and NNTP virtual servers, but should not be used to monitor Exchange Server activity. Because protocol logging is resource and process intensive, Exchange Server would have to perform a lot of extra work to log protocol activity. Instead of choosing all the properties to track, specify only those needed for troubleshooting. Administrators can use logging to determine connection errors, server errors, user authentication errors, protocol command errors, and more. By default, protocol logs are written to the `%SystemRoot%\System32\LogFiles` directory in the format EXYYMMDD.log.

Enabling Protocol Logging

Protocol logging is enabled on each virtual server separately. Whereas HTTP virtual servers are used to track protocol logging for HTTP, OWA, and OMA, SMTP virtual servers are used to track SMTP message submission and transport. To enable protocol logging for SMTP, complete the following steps:

1. In ESM, expand the administrative group of the server you want to work with. Expand Servers, the server to work with, and then expand Protocols.

2. Expand the SMTP node and right-click the virtual server to work with and select Properties.

3. On the General tab, select the check box next to Enable Logging. Select the default log format, W3C Extended Log File Format, unless you're absolutely sure one of the other file formats will fit the logging needs.

4. Click Properties to display a dialog box. On the General tab, the log time interval can be set. Daily or weekly logs will be sufficient in most cases, so select either Daily or Weekly. Use the Log File Directory field to change where the log files will be stored.

5. On the Advanced tab, extended logging options are available. Choose additional properties as needed, click OK, and then click OK again to finish configuring.

Enabling Diagnostic Logging

Diagnostic Logging is used to detect Exchange-related performance issues. Unlike protocol tracking logs that are written to separate log files, diagnostic log files are written to the Window event logs and are viewed through the Application option in Event Viewer. Diagnostic logging can affect server performance, so only enable diagnostic logging when troubleshooting performance issues.

Four levels of logging can be set:

- None—Default level that records only significant events that are written to application, security, and system event logs.

- Minimum—Used to identify a problem that may exist, but does not pinpoint the problem. Exchange records summary entries for each major task.

- Medium—Used to gather more information after a problem is identified. Exchange writes summary and detailed entries in the event logs.

- Maximum—Provides a complete audit trail of every action a service performs. This level severely affects server performance and uses a lot of hard disk space. Monitor hard disk space closely to prevent running out of drive space.

To enable diagnostic logging, perform the following steps:

1. Identify reported performance problems and determine possible services to troubleshoot.

2. In ESM, expand the administrative group of the server you want to work with. Expand Servers, right-click the server to work with, and then select Properties.

3. Click the Diagnostics tab. Use the Services list to select a service(s) to track. The Categories list should show a list of trackable activities, such as replication or authentication.

4. In the Categories list, select the activity to track and then select an appropriate logging level. Repeat this step to track additional activity categories.

5. Repeat steps 3 and 4 to track other services. When you're done, click OK to finish.

Caution When finished troubleshooting, be sure to reset the logging level back to None on any tracked services to prevent hard disk space problems.

Note Remember, if check boxes for settings are grayed out, check the server policy object applied to the server; most likely the server is part of a server policy. To resolve, administrators can disable the policy or remove the server from this policy.

The events are primarily logged in the Application log where key events are recorded by Exchange services. Administrator can access the application through Event Viewer by clicking Start, selecting All Programs or Programs, selecting Administrative Tools, and then pointing to and clicking Event Viewer.

Managing and Troubleshooting Message Queues

Typically, administrators won't see messages in a queue because messages are processed and routed quickly. Messages will remain in the queue if a problem exists. Administrators use the Queue Viewer in System Manager to check for messages in the queue. Queue Viewer provides information helpful for troubleshooting message-flow problems, queue state (Active, Ready, Frozen, and so on), as well as other information such as message submission time or the number of messages waiting in the queue. To locate messages in a queue, use the following steps:

1. In ESM, expand the administrative group of the server you want to work with. Expand Servers, the server to work with, and then select the Queues node to display a list of available queues.

2. Double-click the queue to display the Find Message dialog box and then click Find Now. Search results should be displayed in the Search Results section of the dialog box.

3. Double-clicking a message displays additional information that identifies the message, such as a message ID that can be used with message tracking. Click OK to exit the Message Properties dialog box.

The common problems with queued messages include things such as corruption or viruses. If information is garbled or in an unknown character set when you're viewing message properties, the message is probably corrupt and will need to be deleted. Messages that have multiple deletions and resend attempts are probably infected with a virus and will slow down or stop message queue delivery. Check the originating source of the message and double-check and ensure the virus scanner in use is up-to-date.

If need be, administrators can disable all outbound message delivery directly in the Queue Viewer. Select the queue to work with and then click the Disable Outbound Mail button. This stops outbound mail and give administrators time to troubleshoot and remedy mail problems.

Monitoring Server Health and Performance

Good server health is important to a stable and reliable messaging environment. Using a variety of tools included with Windows 2003 and Exchange 2003, administrators can maximize the uptime of the messaging environment by monitoring items such as memory usage, CPU utilization, SMTP queues, or free disk space.

Using the Performance Console

The Performance Monitor Console (PerfMon) is a toolbox that provides many ways to monitor and analyze server performance issues, network bottlenecks, or gather baselines of server usage. When using Performance Monitor, be methodical and always check these three Windows server resource objects: memory, processor, and disk. After you have checked that they are not causing the bottleneck, check Exchange-specific counters—for example, MSExchangeIS (Send and Receive queues size) and MSExchangeMTA (MSExchangeMTA—Work Queue Length). Some benefits of using PerfMon are understanding what components are doing (for example, is the disk reading or writing most of the time?). Information gathered can be displayed in different formats such as reports and real-time charts or logs, and can help you to know where a minimum investment will produce the maximum gains (such as adding RAM). PerfMon, as shown in Figure 12.2, is launched by selecting Start, All Programs or Programs, Administrative Tools, Performance.

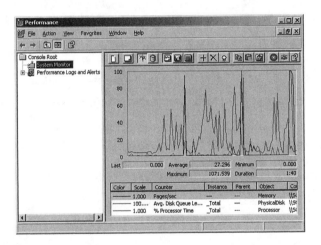

FIGURE 12.2   Viewing server performance in the Performance Monitor Console.

Using Network Monitor

The Network Monitor, as shown in Figure 12.3, is tool that specifically monitors network traffic. Two versions of Network Monitor ship with Microsoft products. The version that comes with Windows Server 2003 is the watered-down version and only allows analysis of traffic sent to or from the server that Network Monitor is running on. The full version of Network Monitor, included with SMS Server, allows monitoring of any machine on your network, determining users' bandwidth consumption and protocol bandwidth consumption, and more. Network Monitor is launched by selecting Start, All Programs or Programs, Administrative Tools, Network Monitor. If prompted, select the network connection to monitor, and then select Capture and click Start.

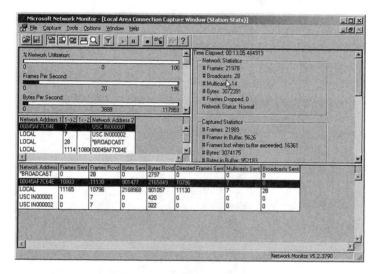

FIGURE 12.3   Viewing network traffic via Network Monitor.

 Tip Network Monitor (NetMon) is not installed by default with Windows 2003, but adding it is easy following these steps:

1. On the Start menu, select Control Panel and then select Add or Remove Programs.

2. Select Add/Remove Windows Components and then choose Management and Monitoring Tools. Click the Details button, select the Network Monitor Tools check box, and then click OK.

> **3.** Follow the instructions until the installation is complete. Administrators can then find NetMon in the Administrative Tools folder (Start Menu, Administrative Tools, Network Monitor).

Using Task Manager

Administrators can get a quick overall idea of how Exchange 2003 is performing at any given time by launching Task Manager: right-click the taskbar and then click Task Manager. Along the top of the Task Manager window are tabs for Applications, Processes, Performance, Networking, and Users. Each tab provides a brief summary of information. The last two tabs were added because of customer requests for information about networking and user-specific attributes. One caveat with Task Manager is that it cannot save historical data—data that is useful for setting baselines and capacity planning.

Monitoring Processor Usage

When CPU utilization is high, Exchange performance suffers greatly. CPU utilization of 100% can be indicative of serious server problems. If a server is stuck at 100% CPU utilization, rebooting is usually necessary to return the server to a functioning level. To keep a check on CPU utilization, configure CPU monitors using the following steps:

1. In ESM, expand the administrative group of the server to work with. Expand Servers, right-click the server to work with, and then select Properties.

2. On the Monitoring tab, click Add. In the Add Resource dialog box, select CPU Utilization and then click OK, displaying the CPU Utilization Thresholds dialog box.

3. Type the number of minutes that must be exceeded to trigger the state change in the Duration (minutes) field. Typically, a value between 5 and 10 minutes should be entered.

4. Configure entries in the Set Maximum CPU Utilization Thresholds section. Select the check box next to Warning State (percent) or Critical State (percent) and then enter values into the associated fields. Typically, a value of 90% is entered for the Warning State threshold and a value of 100% is entered for Critical State threshold.

5. Click OK to finish configuration. If desired, use the following tip to configure automated administrator notification.

 Tip In ESM, right-click the Monitoring and Status folder, click the Notifications subfolder, and select New, Email Notification to create an email notification using built-in scripts. Exchange provides proformas with variables that are substituted with figures at runtime. But wait—isn't the server down? The workaround is to monitor one server from another server. Choose users with mailboxes on different servers so that when a service fails, at least one email notification should get through to an administrator's inbox.

Monitoring Disk Subsystems

In Exchange, free disk space is used for tracking messages, logging, data storage, and virtual memory. Running out of hard disk space will cause data loss and Exchange Server errors. Free disk space should be monitored closely. Configure disk monitoring using the following steps:

1. In ESM, expand the administrative group of the server you want to work with. Expand Servers, right-click the server to work with, and then select Properties.

2. On the Monitoring tab, click Add. In the Add Resource dialog box, select Disk Free Space and then click OK, displaying the Disk Space Thresholds dialog box.

3. Select the drive to monitor, such as C:, in the Drive to Be Monitored drop-down list.

4. Configure entries in the Set Maximum Drive Space Thresholds section. Select the check box next to Warning State (MB) or Critical State (MB) and then enter values in the associated fields. Typically, a value of 500MB is entered for the Warning State threshold and a value of 100MB is entered for Critical State threshold.

5. Click OK to finish configuration. If desired, use the preceding tip to configure automated administrator notification.

Troubleshooting Exchange Databases

When the Exchange databases become corrupt, administrators are typically guided toward two utilities that are shipped with Exchange 2003: `ISINTEG.EXE` and `ESEUTIL.EXE`. ISINTEG and ESEUTIL are powerful tools for ensuring the health of your Exchange information store and to recover from database engine errors. Use these tools with caution when you want to repair your information store and Exchange databases. Be sure a good backup is on hand before using these utilities to check the information store and repair database corruption. Typically, both utilities are located in the `\Program Files\Exchsrvr\Bin directory`.

Using ISINTEG

This tool is used to check and repair the integrity of offline information stores. ISINTEG performs integrity checks on more than 15 database tables searching for logical errors in the information store. The common command-line parameters used for ISINTEG are as follows:

```
isinteg -s SERVERNAME -test allfoldertests
```

Using ESEUTIL

This tool is used for offline defragmentation and compaction of a database, database integrity verification, database repair, and extraction of database file information. ESEUTIL may remove sections of a database in the attempt to repair the database. Use ESEUTIL only as a last resort after trying to restore from backup. The common command-line parameters used for ESEUTIL defragging and repairing are

- Defragmentation—ESEUTIL /d <database name> [options]

  that is, ESEUTIL /d priv1.ebd

- Repair—ESEUTIL /p <database name> [options]

  that is, ESEUTIL /p priv1.ebd

 Caution The /p repair command is a brute force repair method and deletes sections of the database to repair the integrity of the database. The ESEUTIL tool will prompt and require administrators to understand the severity of performing this command. If unsure when prompted, *do not* click OK. Get assistance from someone more experienced before proceeding.

Summary

Proper monitoring and maintenance is essential to a stable, reliable, available Exchange messaging environment. The instructions and processes described throughout this lesson help optimize server performance via troubleshooting and monitoring techniques. By staying on top of the messaging infrastructure using monitoring and maintenance tools, administrators can support an organization's resources more effectively and efficiently, saving time, effort, and costs associated with Exchange Server.

LESSON 13

Backing Up Data Stores with the Windows Server 2003 Backup Utility

This lesson gives an introduction into the basic concepts and methods for backing up data stores and services in Exchange 2003.

Choosing the Proper Backup Regimen

Microsoft Exchange 2003 is used by organizations to store important files and folders of information. When a server crashes, users can potentially lose hours, days, or weeks of work. Administrators are the ones in charge of protecting against data loss and should implement a disaster recovery plan that includes server backup and recovery. A proper backup regimen will help protect against loss of user data, hardware failures, and database corruption.

Creating a backup-and-recovery plan requires planning. Administrators will need to think about their Exchange organization in terms of the number of servers, storage groups, storage group organization, and the number and type of databases per storage group. After the Exchange organization has been planned and mapped out, administrators can prepare a backup-and-recovery plan that includes what data needs to be backed up, how frequently the data needs to be backed up, and so on. Although not a complete list, some items to think about when creating a plan include the following:

- Are the proper hardware, removable disk drives, tape, or optical drives, in place to perform backups?

- When is the best time to schedule backups?

- Where should backups be stored? Should backups include all server software?

- Who is responsible for the backup-and-recovery planning and operation?

- Is one set of data more important than another set?

- How quickly does data need to be recovered? Is a Service Level Agreement needed to ensure a specific server recovery time window?

 Tip Brainstorming in a group setting is a good way to be sure most backup and recovery issues are addressed. This way, everyone responsible can participate in creating a solid backup-and-recovery strategy.

Understanding the Basic Backup Types

There are many methods for backing up data. The methods used are based on factors such as how convenient the backup or recovery process is or the type of data to be backed up.

Online and Offline Backups

Whereas online backups are performed when Exchange services are still running, offline backups are performed when Exchange services are stopped. With online backups and offline backups, Exchange configuration and user data, system state, and file folders containing Windows and

Exchange files can be archived. Typically, online backups are preferred because no interruption to Exchange services is encountered.

Backup Types

Administrators can perform basic types of backups with Exchange 2003:

- Full/Normal backups—All selected Exchange data is archived, including data stores and the current transaction logs. This backup type informs Exchange that a full backup has been performed and to clear out the transaction log files.

- Copy backups—All selected Exchange data is archived, including data stores and the current transaction logs. This backup type does not inform Exchange that a full backup has been performed and to clear out the transaction logs. This allows other backup types to be completed later on.

- Differential backups—Creates backup copies of all data changed since the last normal backup. The actual data stores are not backed up, only the transaction logs are backed up, and the log files are not cleared. Recovering Exchange involves applying the current full backup and then the most recent differential backup.

- Incremental backups—Creates backups of data that has changed since the last normal or incremental backup. The actual data stores are not backed up, only the transaction logs are backed up, and the log files are cleared after the incremental backup is completed. Recovering Exchange involves applying the current full backup and then applying each incremental backup after the full backup.

A typical backup plan will include performing full backups on a weekly basis and supplementing them daily with incremental or differential backups. Be sure to store a backup set offsite in case of an unexpected disaster.

Caution The type of backup depends on the configuration of circular logging. Administrators can specify circular logging settings at the Exchange Storage Group level. Differential or Incremental backups cannot be used if circular logging is enabled. Circular logging allows Exchange to overwrite log files, which prevents reliable restores from the transaction logs.

Understanding Which Components to Back Up

Administrators will want to back up all the server components that will facilitate a complete restore of the server in case the server crashes and must be rebuilt. Using the Windows backup utility called Backup (ntbackup.exe), administrators can create backups on local and remote systems. Using special programming extensions installed with Exchange 2003, Backup can create online backups of Exchange 2003 user and configuration data, system state, and more. Although the first time Backup is used it will start in Wizard mode for ease of use, most administrators will want to use the Advanced mode because it provides more options. The Backup utility can be accessed via the command line by typing **ntbackup.exe** into the Start menu, Run option or by selecting Programs or All Programs, Accessories, System Tools, Backup.

Backing Up Mailbox Data Stores and Public Folder Stores

Administrators can back up Exchange 2003 manually using the Advanced mode of Backup. Configure backups manually by performing the following steps:

1. Start Backup via command line or the Start menu. If Wizard mode is enabled, click Advanced mode and then select the Backup tab as shown in Figure 13.1. Otherwise, just select the Backup tab.

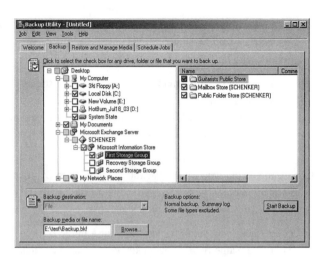

FIGURE 13.1   Using the Backup tab to manually configure a backup set.

2. Clear any existing selections by clicking Job, New on the File menu and selecting Yes when prompted. Choose items to back up by selecting the check boxes next to drives or folders. Selecting a top-level folder will also select all subfolders. Clearing a check box for a top-level folder will also clear subfolder selections.

3. Select backup options for Exchange Server from the following:

   • To create a full backup that includes all Exchange servers in the organization, select the Microsoft Information Store node of each individual server. Expand Microsoft Exchange Server, the server to work with, and then select Microsoft Information Store. Repeat as needed for additional servers.

   • To back up specific servers, expand Microsoft Exchange Server, the server to work with, and then select Microsoft Information Store.

- To back up all user databases on a specific Exchange server, expand Microsoft Exchange Server, the server to work with, and then select Microsoft Information Store.

- To back up specific databases on an Exchange server, expand Microsoft Exchange Server and then the server to work with. Expand Microsoft Information Store, expand the storage group to work with, and then select the database to back up.

4. Choose the media type for the backup in the Backup Destination drop-down list box. The media type may be a file or any existing storage device, such as tape or removable disk.

5. Select the backup media or backup file to use in the Backup Media or File Name field. Type a path and filename or click Browse to find a file. If you're using a tape or removable disk, select the tape or disk to use.

6. Click Start Backup to display the Backup Job Information dialog box, as shown in Figure 13.2. This dialog box contains options for labeling the current backup, appending, or overwriting backup media.

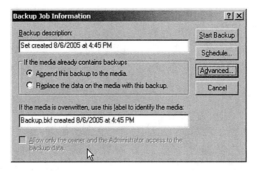

FIGURE 13.2   Using the Backup Job Information dialog box to configure backup settings.

7. To override default settings, click the Advanced button on the Backup Job display box. This dialog box contains options such

as verifying and checking for data errors after backup, compressing backup data to save space, and setting the backup type (normal, copy, differential, or incremental).

8. To schedule the backup for a later date, click the Schedule button on the Backup Job display box. If prompted to save settings, click Yes. Next, type in a descriptive name for the backup selection script and click Save. If prompted for account information, enter administrative account information. Next, type the job name into the Scheduled Job Options dialog box and then click Properties to configure a backup schedule. Skip the remaining step.

9. Click Finish to start the backup. If needed, click Cancel in the Set Information and Backup Progress dialog boxes to stop the backup procedure. When the backup is complete, click Close to edit the process or click Report to view a backup log.

Backing Up Certificate Services

Administrators will also want to back up any Certificate Services on their servers in case of a system crash. The Certificate Authority manages and allocates certificates to users, servers, and workstations when files and folders, email, or network communication need to be secured. For example, Certificate Services are installed on an Exchange server (or a separate server) when an organization wants to use SSL for secured Outlook Web Access. Certificate Services can be backed up along with the system state, but using the Certificate Authority MMC snap-in or command-line utility adds a bit more flexibility when restoring Certificate Services. These options give administrators the benefit of restoring Certificate Services to a previous state without restoring the entire server system state or taking the system offline for the restore. Use the following steps to create a backup of the Certificate Authority (CA):

1. Log on to the CA server using Local Administrator privileges and then create a folder, such as CAbackup, using Windows Explorer on the C: drive.

2. Open Certification Authority on the Start menu by selecting Programs or All Programs, Administrative Tools, Certification Authority. Expand the Certification Authority server and select the appropriate CA.

3. Right-click the CA, point to All Tasks, and then select Back Up CA. Click Next at the CA Backup Wizard screen. On the Items to Back Up page, click the check boxes next to the Private Key and CA Certificate option and the Certificate Database and Certificate Database Log option.

4. Specify the location to store the CA backup files using the folder created in step 1 and then click Next to continue. Enter a password for this file, confirm the password, and click Next to continue.

 Note   To restore the CA private key and CA certificate, the password from step 4 is required. Store the password in a safe and secure location.

5. Click Finish to create the CA backup.

Backing Up Internet Information Services

Administrators will want to back up the Internet Information Services (IIS) that supports the Web and FTP servers. The IIS metabase can be backed up via the system state or using the IIS console. The IIS metabase should be backed up before and after any configuration changes to ensure a successful rollback and to have the latest configuration data backed up after a metabase update. Administrators can back up the metabase via the IIS console using the following steps:

1. Log on to the IIS server using Local Administrator privileges and then open the IIS Manager via the Start Menu by selecting Programs or All Programs, Administrative Tools, Internet Information Services Manager. If the IIS server does not appear, right-click Internet Information Services in the left pane and select Connect. Type in the FQDN of the IIS server and click OK.

2. In the left pane, right-click the IIS server, select All Tasks, and then click Backup/Restore Configuration. The Configuration

Backup/Restore dialog box will display all automatic backups that have been created. Click the Create Backup button.

3. In the Configuration Backup Name field, enter a descriptive name for the backup. If needed, click the Encrypt Backup Using Password check box and provide a password. Click OK when you're finished entering information.

4. The backup will appear in the listing window when the backup is completed. Click Close to return to the IIS console.

Backing Up Active Directory: Users, Groups, and Contacts

Backing up the system state, a collection of system components that depend on each other, creates a point-in-time backup that can be used to restore a server to a previous working state. At the least, system state includes Registry, boot files, and the COM+ registration class. On a domain controller, Active Directory and the SYSVOL share are backed up as part of system state.

Administrators can back up Exchange 2003 manually using the Advanced mode of Backup. Configure backups manually by performing the following steps:

1. Start Backup via command line or the Start menu. If Wizard mode is enabled, click Advanced mode and then select the Backup tab. Otherwise, just select the Backup tab.

2. Clear any existing selections by clicking Job, New on the file menu and selecting Yes when prompted. Select the check box next to the System State node as shown in Figure 13.1.

3. Choose the media type for the backup in the Backup Destination drop-down list box. The media type may be a file or any existing storage device, such as tape or removable disk.

4. Select the backup media or backup file to use in the Backup Media or File Name field. Type a path and filename or click Browse to find a file. If you're using a tape or removable disk, select the tape or disk to use.

5. Click Start Backup to display the Backup Job display box. This dialog box contains options for labeling the current backup, appending, or overwriting backup media.

6. To override default settings, click the Advanced button on the Backup Job display box. This dialog box contains options such as verifying and checking for data errors after backup, compressing backup data to save space, and setting the backup type (normal, copy, differential, or incremental).

7. To schedule the backup for a later date, click the Schedule button on the Backup Job display box. If prompted to save settings, click Yes. Next, type in a descriptive name for the backup selection script and click Save. If prompted for account information, enter administrative account information. Next, type the job name into the Scheduled Job Options dialog box and then click Properties to configure a backup schedule. Skip the remaining step.

8. Click Finish to start the backup. If needed, click Cancel in the Set Information and Backup Progress dialog boxes to stop the backup procedure. When the backup is complete, click Close to end the process or click Report to view a backup log.

Setting Up Recovery Storage Groups

Recovery Storage groups are new to Exchange 2003, a feature that has been in demand by administrators for many years. Recovery Storage Groups facilitate restoring Exchange mailboxes without having to bring up another server or shut down the production email server or restore an entire storage group just to get one single mailbox.

 Caution During the recovery process, transaction and system files are created. These files will require at least as much disk space as the original databases of the mailboxes to be restored. Make sure enough disk space is available before beginning the recovery process.

To create a recovery storage group, use the following steps:

1. In ESM, expand the Servers node and then right-click the server to work with. Point to New on the short menu and then select New Recovery Storage Group.

> **Note**   Remember, the recovery storage group must reside in the same administrative group as the server for which to recover mailboxes.

2. On the Recovery Storage Group Properties page, shown in Figure 13.3, type a descriptive name for the Recovery Storage Group into the Name field.

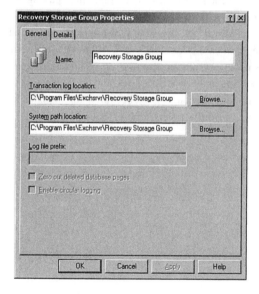

FIGURE 13.3   Creating a Recovery Storage Group in Exchange 2003.

3. The default location for the transaction log and the system path will be automatically set. Use the Browse button to configure alternative file and system path locations.

Caution   Make sure that the system file and transaction log locations are different from the original files. Do not overwrite files!

4. Click OK to create the recovery storage group.

Summary

Backing up an Exchange server is much more than putting in a tape every night and storing the tapes the next day. Good administrators put time and effort into methodically thinking about disaster recovery situations and are totally prepared in case of a server crash. Although a full image backup of the server is necessary, administrators must be prepared to recover individual components and services of a server. Having a tested and documented backup plan as well as good backup media on hand is the first step to recovering from a system failure.

LESSON 14

Restoring Data Stores with the Windows Server 2003 Backup Utility

This lesson introduces the basic concepts and methods for restoring data stores and services in Exchange 2003.

Choosing Which Components to Restore

After a server crash, administrators will want to restore all the server components that facilitate completely restoring the functionality of the server. Using the Restore Wizard or Restore tab within the Windows backup utility called Backup (ntbackup.exe), administrators can restore individual databases and storage groups or restore available backups. Although the first time Backup is used it will start in Wizard mode for ease of use, most administrators will want to use the Advanced mode because it provides more options. The Backup utility can be accessed via command line by typing **ntbackup.exe** in the Start menu, Run option, or by selecting Programs or All Programs, Accessories, System Tools, Backup.

Recovery procedures depend on the types of backups available to administrators. Using normal (full) backups and differential backups, administrators can restore an Exchange database or storage group to the point of failure by performing the following steps:

1. Restore the latest normal backup. Do not set the Last Backup Set option and do not mount the database after the recovery.

2. Restore the latest differential backup. Set the Last Backup Set option and then mount the database after restore to start the replay of the log files.

3. Review the related mailbox and public folder stores to validate a successful recovery of the data.

Using normal backups and incremental backups, administrators can recover an Exchange database or storage group to the point of failure by performing the following steps:

1. Restore the latest normal backup. Do not set the Last Backup Set option and do not mount the database after the recovery.

2. In order, apply each incremental backup. Restore the first incremental backup after the full backup, then restore the second incremental backup, and so on until incremental backups have been restored.

3. When restoring the last incremental backup, be sure to set the Set the Last Backup Set option and then mount the database after restore to start the replay of the log files.

4. Review the related mailbox and public folder stores to validate a successful recovery of the data.

Restoring Mailboxes and Public Folders

Administrators can restore Exchange 2003 data manually using the Advanced mode of Backup. Configure backups manually by performing the following steps:

1. Recover system and configuration before restoring user data. Server documentation should include the following steps:

    • Stop all Exchange and IIS services when restoring config-uration data. After exiting Exchange System Manager,

restart ESM and then restart the Microsoft Exchange
Information Store via the Service program in
Administrative Tools.

- Dismount the affected data stores before starting the
  restore of user data. During restore, Exchange Services are
  temporarily stopped.

- Restore the drives, system state data, Exchange configuration data, and Exchange user data when recovering an
  entire server.

2. Start Backup via command line or the Start menu. If Wizard
   mode is enabled, click Advanced mode and then select the
   Restore and Manage Media tab as shown in Figure 14.1.
   Otherwise, select the Restore and Manage Media tab.

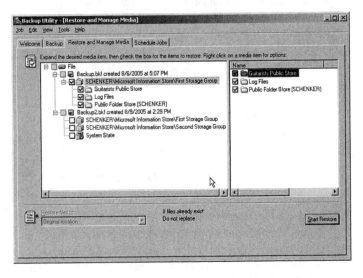

FIGURE 14.1 Using the Restore and Manage Media tab to manually configure a restore operation.

3. Select the data to restore using the left pane view, which displays files organized by volume, and the right pane view, which
   displays media sets. If no media set is displayed, right-click File

in the left pane view, select Catalog File, and then enter the path for the backup file.

4. To recover Exchange data, individually select the Information Store storage groups to restore. To restore an individual mailbox store or log files for a storage group, expand the storage group node and then select the appropriate mailbox store and log files. If no file data or system state is to be recovered, skip to step 6. Otherwise, continue to step 5.

5. To recover file data, select the check box next to any drive, folder, or file to restore. Exchange data and file data cannot be restored in the same recovery operation. Typically, file data will be recovered first and then Exchange data.

6. Administrators can specify how to restore files by clicking Tools and selecting Options on the menu bar. The Options dialog box opens, displaying the Restore tab. Available options are as follows:

   • Do Not Replace the Files on My Computer (Recommended)—Selecting this option does not overwrite existing files.

   • Replace the File on Disk Only if the File on Disk Is Older—Selecting this option replaces older files on the disk with newer files from backup.

   • Always Replace the File on My Computer—Selecting this option replaces all files on disk with files from the backup.

7. Use the Restore File To drop-down list to specify the restore location. The Original location option restores data to the folder or files logged during the backup process. The Alternate Location option restores data to the administrator-specified location while preserving the existing directory structure. The Single Folder option restores all data to an administrator-specified single folder without keeping the existing directory structure.

8. Click Restore to display the Restoring Database dialog box. In the Restore To field, type the name of the server to restore files to, such as **Schenker**, or click Browse to search for a computer.

9. If this is the last backup set to restore, select the check boxes next to the Last Backup Set and Mount Database After Restore options. Click OK to start restoring data. If prompted, type in a name of the backup set to use. If needed, click Cancel in the Operation Status and Restore Progress dialog boxes to stop the recovery process. When the restore is complete, click Close to complete the process or click Report to view a backup log containing information about the restore operation.

Be sure to complete post-recovery checklist items of mailbox and public folder stores to ensure that data recovery was successful.

Restoring Certificate Services

Administrators will often want or need to restore Certificate Services. This procedure is useful if you want to restore a Certification Authority (CA) without restoring the entire server on which the CA is installed. Using the Windows interface, perform the following steps to restore the CA:

1. Log on to the system as a Backup Operator or a Certification Authority Administrator.

2. Open Certification Authority on the Start menu by selecting Programs or All Programs, Administrative Tools, Certification Authority. Expand the Certification Authority server and select the appropriate CA.

3. Right-click the CA, point to All Tasks, and then select Restore CA. If prompted by the Certificate Services Wizard to stop Certificate Services, click OK to do so and then click Next at the wizard welcome page.

4. On the Items to Restore page, click the check boxes next to the items to restore (Private Key and CA Certificate or Certificate Database and Certificate Database Log), click Browse to locate the directory containing the backup files, such as CAbackup, and then click Next to continue.

5. On the Password page, enter the password that was entered during the backup process. If the password is correct, the

Certification Authority Restore Wizard dialog box will be displayed as shown in Figure 14.2.

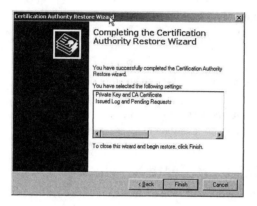

FIGURE 14.2   Viewing CA restore results on the Certification Authority Restore Wizard dialog box.

Restoring Internet Information Services

Restoring the Internet Information Service (IIS) configuration may be necessary if IIS metabase data info is erased, becomes corrupt, or is not functioning as desired. Use the following steps to restore the IIS metabase data:

1. Log on to the IIS server using Local Administrator privileges and then open the IIS Manager via the Start menu by selecting Programs or All Programs, Administrative Tools, Internet Information Services Manager. If the IIS server does not appear, right-click Internet Information Services in the left pane and select Connect. Type in the FQDN of the IIS server and click OK.

2. In the left pane, right-click the IIS server and select All Tasks; then click Backup/Restore Configuration. The Configuration Backup/Restore window will display all automatic backups that have been created. Select the backup to use and then click the Restore button to perform a manual restore.

3. A dialog box will pop up stating that all Internet services need to be stopped prior to restoring the data and will be restarted when the restore is complete. Click Yes to continue the restore.

4. A confirmation will be displayed when the restore is completed. When you're finished reviewing, click OK to close the window. Click Close on the Configuration Backup/Restore page.

5. In IIS Manager, verify that the restore was successful and that services are up and running. Close IIS Manager and log off the server.

 Note By default, backups are stored in the `%systemroot%\system32\Inetsrv\MetaBack` directory.

IIS Web and FTP folders are located in the `C:\InetPub\` directory and the IIS log files are located in `C:\Windows\system32\LogFiles`. To recover the IIS website, the IIS Logs, or the FTP site, restore the files using the Backup utility.

Restoring Active Directory: Users, Groups, and Contacts

Administrators can back up Exchange 2003 manually using the Advanced mode of Backup. Configure backups manually by performing the following steps:

1. Follow steps 1–3 in the instructions for recovering mailbox and public folder data found in the "Restoring Mailboxes and Public Folders" section of this lesson.

2. To restore system state data, select the System State check box and check boxes for other data to recover. If data is being restored to the original location, the current system state is replaced by the system state being restored. If the system state is restored to an alternate location, only SYSVOL, system boot files, and Registry information is restored; system state data can be restored only on a local system.

By default, Active Directory and other replicated data such as SYSVOL are not restored on a domain controller. This protects the AD information on the domain controller by preventing the domain information from being overwritten.

3. Follow the remaining steps 5–9 of the instructions for recovering mailbox and public folder data found in the "Restoring Mailboxes and Public Folders" section.

Be sure to complete the post-recovery checklist items of the system state and any other restored data to ensure that data recovery was successful.

Using Recovery Storage Groups

A Recovery Storage group is created on an Exchange 2003 server in an Administration group where the original databases reside. Use the following instructions to recover Exchange data using Recovery Storage groups:

1. Use the instructions for creating a Recovery Storage group as outlined in the section "Setting Up Recovery Storage Groups" in Lesson 13, "Backing Up Data Stores with the Windows Server 2003 Backup Utility."

2. Right-click the recovery group container and select Add Database to Recover. The Select Database to Recover dialog box is displayed, as shown in Figure 14.3. Select the mailbox store to recover and then click OK.

3. Start the tape backup software in use, such as NTBackup, and restore the database to recover into a temporary directory. When the restore is complete, right-click the mailbox store in the Recovery Storage group and select Mount Store.

4. Click Start, select Run. Type the path of the ExMerge.exe, which should be %ProgramFiles%\Exchsrvr\Bin\ExMerge, to use the Microsoft Exchange Mailbox Merge Wizard to select mailboxes

and restore them, merging data from the recovery databases with the existing data of the original databases. Click OK to initiate ExMerge.

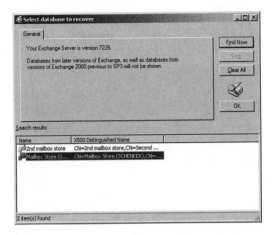

FIGURE 14.3 Selecting a mailbox store for recovery in the Add Database to Recover option.

 The Exchange Mailbox Merge Wizard may need to be installed. Administrators can download the software from Microsoft at http://www.microsoft.com/technet/ prodtechnol/exchange/downloads/default.mspx, or they can copy the files from the Exchange 2003 CD ROM directory, `\Support\Utils\I386\ExMerge`, onto the Exchange server in the directory, `\Program Files\ Exchsrvr\Bin`. The following files should then be available for use in the directory: `ExMerge.exe`, `ExMerge.ini`, `ExMerge.rtf`.

5. Click Next, select Extract or Import (One Step Procedure) and then click Next again to get to the Source Server page, as shown in Figure 14.4.

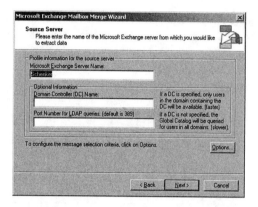

FIGURE 14.4   Specifying the source server that the Recovery Storage group was created on via the Microsoft Exchange Mailbox Merge Wizard.

6. Click the Options button to display the Data Selection Criteria dialog box. The option specifies what data to export and how the data should be handled. There are five tabs:

    • Data—Use this option to specify which data from the source store to use.

    • Import—Use the option to specify whether to merge, copy, archive, or replace data.

    • Folders—Use this option to specify folders that should be processed.

    • Dates—Use this option to specify whether the message date should be used to filter messages.

    • Message Details—Use this option to specify the exact message subject or filename of attachments to look for.

    Click OK when you're finished making changes or to accept the defaults.

7. Click Next. On the Destination Server Wizard page, type in the name of the destination server in the server field. This should be

the name of the original server from which the original backup was made. Click Next to continue.

8. On the Database Selection Wizard page, select the Recovery Storage group to work with and then click Next.

9. On the Mailbox Selection Wizard page, choose the mailboxes to recover and then click Next. Multiple mailboxes can be chosen by using the Shift and Ctrl keys to select multiple mailboxes.

10. On the Local Selection Wizard page, select the default language to use when connecting to a mail box that has not yet been created. This also controls the language used for the default folders of any mailbox that is created. Click Next to continue.

11. On the Target Directory Wizard page, select the drive and subdirectory where mailbox PST files should be extracted to and then click Next. Be sure that adequate disk space is available by reviewing the Disk Space Required field value.

12. If saving the current settings for future usage is desired, click Save Settings and then click Next. Otherwise, just click Next.

13. Click Finish. The ExMerge wizard exports the data into PST files and then imports the data into the selected mailboxes.

If errors occur, check the `ExMerge.log` file, located in the `\Program Files\Exchsrvr\Bin` directory. The log file will contain information helpful for troubleshooting and resolving errors.

When you're finished using the Recovery Storage group, right-click the mounted database and select Dismount Store. Confirm the action by clicking Yes. This will dismount the recovery database and allow normal recovery operations of the Exchange Server to resume. Also, be sure to complete post-recovery checklist items of restored data to ensure that data recovery was successful.

Summary

Disaster recovery in Exchange 2003 involves a variety of different options. Although an entire server recovery can be performed, other recovery options are available for recovering information that was lost because of data corruption, file, or message deletion due to user error. Using extensive server documentation, tools, and wizards such as NTBACKUP, Mailbox Move, and ExMerge, or new features, such as Recovery Storage groups, administrators can recover from a variety of data loss situations by using the correct tool for the task. This way, administrators can maximize the amount of server availability for end users by resolving Exchange Server-related problems quickly!

LESSON 15

Exploring Exchange 2003 Tools, Resources, and Links

This lesson explores some of the various tools, resources, and websites available in the Exchange support community.

Help! Where Can I Go?

Now that we have looked at the what, why, and how of Exchange Server 2003 along with some of the new features of Outlook 2003 and Windows 2003, I want to show you some of the things I have experienced in working with Exchange Server 2003 over the past couple of years. By no means is the information covered in this lesson the only choice when dealing with Exchange Server, but it gives you avenues to explore when looking for third-party products and support.

We will take a look at four main areas:

- Backup tools—Third-party archiving products for Exchange 2003.

- Antivirus utilities—Third-party antivirus products for Exchange 2003.

- Antispam utilities—Third-party antispam products for Exchange 2003.

- The Online Exchange Server Community—Who, what, and where of the online support community for Exchange 2003.

Information in this lesson, including URLs and website references, may change without notice. I've tried to include only those references that I believe will be around for the long haul. I have no control over the resources and links and therefore cannot prevent them from changing. If they do change, there is a good chance that you will still be able to locate them on the Internet:

- Old links may refer you to the new site.

- A parent site may provide new links to the information.

- Use search tools such as MSN Search, Google, or Yahoo to locate information.

If all else fails, try the Wayback Machine at the Internet Archive (http://www.archive.org). The Wayback Machine is an Internet time machine that provides the capability to access and browse stored archives of web pages and sites. Give it a try, it's pretty cool!

Backup Tools

Third-party backup programs provide advanced archiving capabilities. With the introduction of Windows Server 2003 and Volume Shadow Copy Service (VSCS), backup software companies and administrators can worry a little less about disaster recovery. Using point-in-time snapshots of data, backups can be performed while leaving Exchange Server online. They provide the next level of backup and recovery and add enhanced functionality not found in Windows Backup.

Although the Windows Backup can be used to perform backups of Exchange Server, it does not support backing up Exchange with VSCS. Administrators will need to purchase a backup product from a vendor such as Veritas to support using VSCS.

VERITAS Backup Exec

Backup Exec for Windows Servers in conjunction with VERITAS Backup Exec Agent for Exchange Server provides protection for Exchange 2003 data while the Stores are online. The Backup Agent for Exchange provides backups and restores of all Exchange data. In addition, mailbox or message-level restores from a full traditional backup do not require installation of a separate Exchange 2003 server. When running on Microsoft Windows Server 2003, the Backup Exec Agent for Exchange Server supports Volume Snapshot (VSS) technology, allowing the user the option of selecting either the VERITAS or the Microsoft Volume Shadow Copy Service technology for protecting open files.

CommVault Galaxy Backup and Recovery

Galaxy Backup and Recovery for Microsoft Exchange 2000/2003 is CommVault's (www.commvault.com) enterprise archiving solution for protecting Exchange 2003 data. The CommVault Galaxy iDataAgent for Exchange provides a centralized and automated backup/recovery. Similar to VERITAS Backup Exec, Galaxy leverages Microsoft's Single Instance Store and scales to support large enterprise organizations. Galaxy leverages VSS (software and hardware), allowing a single system to manage Exchange data across the enterprise.

Antivirus Utilities

As malicious virus writers continue to create and release new viruses, worms, Trojans, and other malicious code into the data and networking world, antivirus companies are working hard to create new approaches to traditional prevention techniques. The new VSAPI version 2.5 in Exchange 2003 provides better interaction when a virus is found and also allows virus scanning applications to scan for viruses throughout the organization on different types of Exchange servers, such as front-end servers and bridgehead servers, instead of just servers hosting Exchange mailboxes.

> Unsure if your current antivirus product supports
> VSAPI? Consult your product documentation and
> check the Registry key at `HKEY_LOCAL_MACHINE\System\`
> `CurrentControlSet\Services\MSExchangeIS\VirusScan`.
> If an entry is present, your current antivirus software
> is using the VSAPI. If not, you should consider upgrad-
> ing your antivirus software to improve email scanning
> performance and security.

Sybari Antigen for Exchange

A subsidiary of Microsoft, Sybari (www.sybari.com) provides a robust
solution for virus scanning in the enterprise. Antigen for Microsoft
Exchange supplies a layered protection solution that offers a solid defense
against undesirable traffic. Antigen also minimizes worm-generated spam
and safeguards the Information Store through the proprietary Antigen
Worm Purge technology.

Symantec Mail Security for Microsoft Exchange

Symantec (www.symantec.com) provides an integrated security solution
that protects against viruses, Trojans, worms, and other unwanted content.
Symantec Mail Security for Microsoft Exchange uses proprietary
NAVEXTM antivirus technology that defends against new and known
viruses. Via the integrated LiveUpdate feature, updated virus definitions
can be deployed enterprisewide without stopping scan services or incur-
ring server downtime.

McAfee GroupShield for Microsoft Exchange

McAfee (www.mcafee.com) provides proactive security solutions that
protect network and system infrastructure from zero-day threats (attacks
that take advantage of software vulnerabilities for which there are no
available fixes) such as viruses, Trojans, and worms. As part of the
McAfee Protection-in-Depth Strategy, GroupShield for Exchange protects

Microsoft Exchange Server 2003 environments from all types of malicious email-borne threats.

Panda Exchange Secure Antivirus

Panda Software (www.pandasoftware.com) provides a complete antivirus for Microsoft groupware servers. Their flagship antivirus product for Exchange 2003, Panda Antivirus for Exchange Server, scans and disinfects all inbound and outbound corporate email traffic in real-time and blocks malicious content before it reaches the recipient's mailbox.

Trend Micro ScanMail for Microsoft Exchange

Trend Micro's (www.trendmicro.com) ScanMail for Microsoft Exchange guards against viruses, Trojans, worms, and other malicious code hidden in email. By filtering inbound/outbound email traffic at the SMTP connector-level, ScanMail blocks threats before they can enter or leave the mail server, protecting end users from unwanted email content.

AntiSpam Utilities

Industry analyst Gartner Inc. claims that up to 50% of the average business mailbox is spam! It is quickly becoming a potential legal liability and a major productivity drain for corporate IT departments and end users. To help combat the onslaught of unwanted inbound email, lost productivity, consumption of communication bandwidth, and drain of technical support, many companies have created add-in and standalone software to prevent the delivery of spam to end user mailboxes.

iHateSpam Server Edition

iHateSpam, by Sunbelt Software (www.sunbelt-software.com), is a Microsoft Exchange add-in; it requires Exchange Server. iHateSpam operates on and integrates with the server using the Exchange user directory for the iHateSpam directory. The management interface will be familiar to administrators, minimizing the learning curve. iHateSpam version 1.7 utilizes two spam filter engines, allowing administrators to choose the

Sunbelt Software antispam Engine only or the Cloudmark Antispam Engine only. For maximum effectiveness, both engines can and should be used.

Lyris MailShield

Lyris MailShield Server (www.lyris.com) is a server-based email filtering program for medium- and large-sized businesses. MailShield Server can be used to block spam, prohibit mail relaying, and prevent mail bomb attacks. The server-based application also includes a searchable incoming and outgoing email audit trail, which helps organizations deal with legal issues and compliance issues associated with inappropriate and unacceptable email messages.

SpamArrest.com

Spam Arrest's enterprise solution is an easy and cost-effective way for organizations to protect against unwanted spam. Using Spam Arrest protection services, all incoming email messages sent to an organization's domain are first routed to Spam Arrest's datacenter servers. Messages sent to protected accounts are processed at Spam Arrest and only messages from verified senders are forwarded to your SMTP server. Otherwise, nonprotected email is immediately forwarded to the organization's SMTP server. This solution is good for organizations looking to minimize in-house hardware needs.

Tapping into the Online Exchange Server Community

The online Exchange support community is a large and thriving worldwide support base fed by websites, forums, and web logs. All of these sources of information encompass the vast amount of experience and expertise available on Exchange 2003. The online community is a good place to start when looking for help troubleshooting and resolving issues related to Exchange 2003.

The Experts Exchange Website

Experts Exchange (www.experts-exchange.com) is a website that provides IT technical support on a variety of technologies. Technical problems related to Exchange can be posted on the site in the appropriate Exchange section and Exchange experts post technical solutions based on experience and known solutions. Administrators can search the site using error messages or verbal descriptions and then browse potential solutions. (Look for my technical editor, Paul Clement, and me on the site!)

The Slip Stick Website

Slipstick Systems (www.slipstick.com) is another website directed at administrators and power users. This site contains information on the latest Outlook and Exchange Service Packs, solutions to common problems, and information on security holes. The site is filled with how-to articles, links to useful add-ins, tools, and related Outlook and Exchange hot topics.

The MS Exchange.org Website

MSExchange.org is a well-organized resource site for Microsoft Exchange Server news, downloads, tutorials, how-to articles, and FAQs. The website also includes information regarding third-party Exchange and Outlook products and add-ons.

The Microsoft Exchange Product Home Page

The best place to start for Exchange-related information, tools, downloads, and more is at the Microsoft Exchange Product home page at http://www.microsoft.com/exchange. Administrators will find links to other Microsoft Exchange-related sites, such as the Exchange Server 2003 TechCenter, trial downloads of Exchange 2003, and other items such as Exchange service packs.

The Microsoft Exchange Server 2003 Support Center

The Microsoft Exchange Server 2003 support center, shown in Figure 15.1, can be found on the web at http://support.microsoft.com/exch2003. This site contains official Microsoft how-to articles, downloads, and troubleshooting techniques for Exchange 2003. It also has official links to the most recent knowledgebase articles, related sites such as the Exchange Community Newsgroups, and additional support resources such as On Demand Messaging Webcasts.

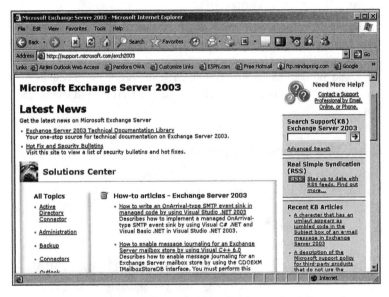

FIGURE 15.1   Viewing information available on the Microsoft Exchange Server 2003 support center.

The Exchange Server Developer Center

The Exchange Server Developer Center, located on the Web at http://msdn.microsoft.com/exchange, is the primary site for application development organizations. It is the best source for the latest release of the

Exchange 2003 Software Development Kit (SDK) for developers building applications for Exchange 2003. The page also contains downloadable samples of code written in C#, C++, VB .NET, and VBScript.

The Exchange Server TechCenter

The Exchange Server TechCenter is designed to help administrators connect with Exchange Server-related resources from Microsoft and also the broader Exchange Server community. This website can be found at http://www.microsoft.com/technet/exchange/. The site provides access to the top Exchange stories, tasks, and downloads. The site also includes top-notch technical documentation in the form of knowledgebase articles and reference materials related to migrations, planning and deployment, upgrading, and security. The information on this page has been reviewed and validated by the Microsoft Exchange Server team.

The Microsoft Knowledge Base

As shown in Figure 15.2, the Microsoft Knowledge Base online, located at http://support.microsoft.com/search, is a web front-end interface to Microsoft's database of Knowledge Base articles, policies, and how-to articles. As you have seen throughout this book, Knowledge Base articles (also known as KBs) can be quite useful for troubleshooting. Because they are updated frequently, they often contain information about Exchange that may not have been published yet in other Exchange product documentation.

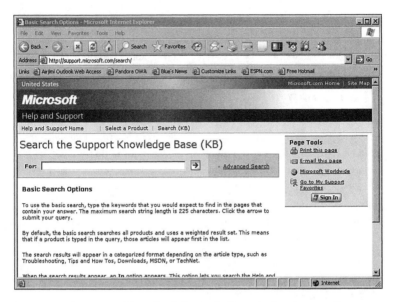

FIGURE 15.2 Searching the Microsoft Knowledge Base online using Internet Explorer.

Summary

The Internet is a huge resource for Exchange information related to planning, deployment, administration, and troubleshooting. Administrators can research information about third-party backup and restore applications, antivirus, and antispam prevention products. The online community in support of Exchange 2003 is huge and contains a large library of expertise and information available to administrators with a few keystrokes on their keyboard. In addition to the Exchange 2003 product home page, Microsoft has several other home pages with Exchange-related content geared toward IT professionals and application developers.

INDEX

F

G

N - O

X - Y - Z

Your Guide to Computer Technology

www.informit.com